# The Leader's Mental Scorecard
### Discover Your Leadership Sweet Spot

Dear Janet!

Leadership for more pleasure
and less pain.

# The Leader's Mental Scorecard - Discover Your Leadership Sweet Spot

Book cover and design by: Ida Bjørnstrøm
Illustrations: Garuda Research Institute
Drawings: Morten Ingemann
Printed by: Børge Møllers Grafiske hus, Aarhus

Original title: Lederens Mentale Scorekort
Translation: Dee Shields
1st edition, 1st impression, September 2005

ISBN: 87-989537-1-0

Published by Garuda Forlag


www.garudahr.com
www.golfersprofile.com
www.mental-scorecard.com

Finn Havaleschka

# The Leader's Mental Scorecard
## Discover Your Leadership Sweet Spot

Garuda Research Institute
Providing People with Opportunities

## By the Same Author

Vejen til Jobbet, 1981

Om at vælge rigtigt, 1982

Lederes Personlighed, 1989
*English Edition:*
The Personality of the Leader, 1997

Lederens vej - fra viden til visdom, 1990
*English Edition:*
In Search of Leadership, 1997

Lederskab og Personlighed, 1991

Din Profil, 1991
*Swedish Edition:*
Din Personlighet, 1992

Personality and Leadership - a Benchmark Study of Success and Failure, 1995

The Leader's Choice, 1997

Om... Udvikling, Livet og Ledelse, 1997
*English Edition:*
On... Development, Life and Leadership

Golferens Mentale Scorekort
*English Edition:*
The Golfer's Mental Scorecard, 2003

# Contents

# Foreword

## Leader, Know Thyself

By Associate Professor Nils Villemoes, Department of Management and International Business, Aarhus School of Business, Denmark.

In his novel "A Fugitive Crosses His Tracks," Danish/Norwegian author Aksel Sandemose walks around the base of a mountain while philosophizing about how the mountain changes countenance as he walks around it. Suddenly, the light falls upon it in a new way, creating a new mountain. That's the way it is with all of existence: it seems different, depending on where we are and what color glasses we are wearing while gazing upon it. It is true as it is written: that there is nothing new under the sun. Luckily, though, the sun does move around a bit, shedding new light on what we are examining…

As far as leadership is concerned, there are truly many points of view – 27, at least. However, we can group them into three categories, which makes it somewhat easier for us to contemplate them.

1. The open perspective has to do with the relationship between surroundings, customers, the market and the future. It is a question of STRATEGY.
2. The purpose of the rational perspective is to make the best possible use of the resources available   time, money, people, etc. It is a question of ORGANIZATION.
3. The so-called "natural" perspective is aimed at behavior, motivation, communication and cooperation: in Greek, SYNERGY.

These three perspectives also appear in psychology, e.g. in Freud's works: the id, the ego and the superego. It is these three forces that keep us going but also keep us within certain behavioral boundaries: Behave yourself! This is leadership on a personal level.

Finn Havaleschka has been working with these dimensions of leadership for many, many years. He philosophizes over their meaning, but he doesn't stop at philosophizing, as so many do. He measures and tests everyone that crosses his path, both in relation to the three perspectives mentioned above, but also in relation to a fourth dimension, which in a certain sense is the most important one: the issue of obtaining results.

- Good leaders know what they want, use their heads, set a goal and then go for it.
- Good leaders understand and use the resources available to them and have a well-organized box of tools to do it with.
- Good leaders are accessible and present: they listen, get involved, are interested in their subordinates, and their heart is in it.
- Good leaders get something out of their endeavors, carry out their plans, and do their legwork properly.

These four roles or viewpoints are four ways to be a leader. Finn has tested thousands of leaders based on these dimensions and has gathered an impressive amount of data. He's been around the mountain many times.

Now he's sitting back in his comfy chair, lighting a cigar and asking himself – and us – a series of good questions. What has happened in leadership over the past 25-30 years? Have all our attempts to develop good leaders borne any fruit? Have we become more flexible, more mobile, and more willing to take risks? Do we think more in holistic terms than we used to? These are good questions!

Finn also asks whether there are differences between men and women when it comes to leadership, an issue guaranteed to make most women sit up and notice.

Can we learn to lead, or is it in our biology? Is a certain enzyme – dopamine – what controls our desire and ability to make decisions? What role does upbringing play in this connection? It's a given that some people would rather not have to be leaders; then they have to accept others taking on that role. What are we leading for? That's another good question Finn asks in his book.

It would be wrong of me to reveal the answers given in the book. Neither is the purpose of the book to end the discussion with a few incontrovertible truths. The idea is to keep the pot boiling and to inspire the reader to keep on walking around the mountain. Explore your own personal leadership universe. There are many points of view out there we have yet to discover...

The Leader's Mental Scorecard. © Finn Havaleschka.

# Preface

## Why Spend Time Learning About the Ways of Danish Leadership

As a Dane my mother tongue is Danish, a language shared only by some 5 million people. As founder of a management company with partners in most parts of the world, all our personality tests, concepts and management tools, i.e. all my intellectual work, has to be translated into English, and then into the partners local language, for example Japanese and Italian. The same goes for this book too. But translating and publishing a book of this volume costs money. So naturally it's an investment on which I like to get a return. But what should make you and other potential readers, who probably do not know much about Denmark or Danish leadership, purchase the book? While I was working on the book, and also pondering about this question, several surveys made by highly recognized institutions and scholars were published. All of them placing Denmark remarkably high when it came to issues such as welfare, quality of life, job satisfaction, economic competitiveness, public governance and innovation et cetera.

Reading the results of the surveys, I asked myself: is this really true, are we that unique? Thinking about it, the answer is yes. During the last 10 years or so, I have been traveling in many parts of the world in order to establish and train new Garuda Partners. These activities have given me plenty of opportunities to discuss the subject of leadership and leadership development and to compare differences in leadership style, attitudes and values in different cultures. This experience confirms not only that the results of the surveys are factual, but most important, that the facts are a result or consequences of the Danish culture. A culture with values and attitudes formed and developed over the past thousand years, since the time when the Vikings went out into the world to explore the opportunities for trade and survival. The Danish culture is unique (as are all other cultures), but the uniqueness of our culture forms the foundation or platform, from which we have evolved to be one of the richest countries in the world with no less than 76% of the population stating that they are very satisfied with their jobs, career opportunities and the way they are managed.

But it should be mentioned that it is not part of the Danish culture to flaunt ones success and uniqueness publicly. Even if you are really unique and/or very successful, it is not popular to show it or talk about it. This attitude is called The Law of Jante, and is defined as a set of views that scorns individual success and those who set themselves above others. Now, I have meet many people around the world who have asked me how Denmark could become so rich and the population so satisfied. Diverting from the Law of Jante, the answer lies in the culture and the tradition of leadership that is a consequence or a product of the culture.

This book is not a book about Danish culture, but a presentation of a leadership concept that is a product of the culture. In the following you can read about the welfare, quality of life, job satisfaction and creativity this way of managing people can lead to. It is my hope that this perspective for you and your leadership will induce you to purchase and practice what you read in the book. Now to the facts.

## Background

Denmark is a small country, with its population of 5 million its only raw material resource, yet (or perhaps for exactly that reason) Denmark is one of the richest, most competitive and innovative countries in the world. My point is that it is perhaps exactly this lack of rich natural resources that laid the foundation for a culture in which leadership at all levels is applied to finding, developing and utilizing the skills and resources of each individual citizen and employee. Many studies indicate that it is leadership that makes the difference.

## Return on Investment, Innovation and Competitive Ability

The *Economist Intelligence Unit*, the business intelligence institute of The *Economist Group*[1], claims that Denmark is now and will be for the next five years the world's best country to invest in. The *European Policy Centre*[2] has nominated Denmark the world leader in economic competitiveness, listing

---

[1]  Economist Intelligence Unit of The Economist Group. "Denmark economy: Top of the class." 1 April 2005 <http://www.viewswire.com/index.asp?layout=display_article&doc_id=978174297>.
[2]  Clees, Nick. "Why Europe should look within for inspiration. *Financial Times*. 31 March 2005."

reasons such as the country's development investment, high technology, telecommunications, strong labor market, and physical and social infrastructure. The *World Bank*[3] views good governance as a key factor to welfare and economic growth. In the latest survey (April 2005) Denmark is ranked number one in the world in this category.

## Motivation, Involvement and Responsibility

A StepStone ASA[4] survey shows that, more than other Europeans, Danes believe that they make a difference and benefit the company they work for. Most Danish employees feel that their work is valued and that their superiors praise and motivate them. A PLS Ramboel/ISR[5] report found that 76% of all Danes are satisfied with their jobs, 83% indicating that the main reason they feel this way is that they are permitted to exercise an influence and are given responsibility.

## Quality of Life, Individualism and Power Distance

In his book *Happiness: Lessons from a New Science*[6], author Richard Layard concludes, on the basis of an extensive study, that the population of Denmark are the happiest people in the world. One of the primary sources of this happiness is their relationships with other people, including superior-subordinate relationships. Analyses by Professor Geert Hofstedes[7] reveal the nature of these relationships. The power distance, i.e. the distance from subordinate to leader, is short and direct, and a high degree of individualism is encouraged, and this is reflected in the responsibilities employees are given. In addition, the traditional masculine role model is assigned a lower priority today, which means that diversity and change are permitted more than previously.

---

[3]   <http://www.worldbank.org/wbi/governance/>.
[4]   StepStone ASA. "European Companies Value Their Employees' Work". 23 February 2005 <http://www.stepstone.com/news_detail.cfm?aid=197>.
[5]   NAP 2002. "The Government: Denmark's National Action Plan for Employment 2002." <http://www.bm.dk/english/publications/napuk2002/NAP2002-eng.pdf>.
[6]   Layard, Richard. *Happiness: Lessons from a New Science*. New York. The Penguin Press, 2005.
[7]   Hofstede, Geert. *Cultures' Consequences*. Newbury Park, California. Sage Publications: *Cultures and Organizations: Software of the Mind*. New York. McGraw-Hill, 1991. <www.geert-hofstede.com>.

The Leader's Mental Scorecard. © Finn Havaleschka.

## Dinosaur Leadership

In their 1982 book *In Search of Excellence*[8], authors Peters and Waterman critique what I call "dinosaur leadership". They found that positive reinforcement was more important: in other words, motivation instead of force. This was a realization that Danish management circles had come to a long time before Peters and Waterman embarked upon their careers. But it was also known that motivation must rest upon a reliable foundation of trust and balance between people, between superior and subordinate, between politician and citizen, and between government authorities and individual citizens.

## Creativity and Innovation

The level of trust and influence and responsibility delegated to subordinates might also be one of the factors behind Professor Richard Florida's ranking of Denmark as number six in the world when it comes to creativity and innovation[9]. Trust people and give them the freedom to make mistakes, seems to be the key to success for Public Governance as well as for private.

## Leader, Know Thyself

In the foreword, Professor Nils Villemoes gives us a good idea of the foundation of leadership in Denmark. Leadership is about developing personal skills and the ability to look at things from other points of view, to observe and reflect upon before reaching new realizations. Nor is there anything new about this: it was expressed as early as the 1800s, when Danish philosopher Søren Kierkegaard wrote:

> If I am to succeed in leading a person towards a certain goal, then I must first find my way to the place where this person is, and start right there.

---

[8] Peters, T.J. & Waterman, R.H. "Man Waiting for Motivation." *In Search of Excellence.* London. Harper Business, 1982.

[9] Florida, R. *"The Flight of the Creative Class: The New Global Competition for Talent."* NY. NY. Harper business, April, 2005. <www.creativeclass.org.>

Kierkegaard realized that things were not always so easy. As human beings, we prefer to take our starting point in our own point of view, in our own values, attitudes and beliefs. For this reason, he added the following:

You have to dare to lose your foothold to move forward.

The leadership model introduced in this book is an excellent expression and continuation of the Danish management tradition. If as a leader (at any level), you wish to create growth and utilize the full potential of the nation and of the individual organization, reflection and change must begin in the leader him/herself. It starts with finding out where you stand, then where your subordinates stand, and then how you – by daring to lose your foothold – can move to the place where your subordinates stand.

I am convinced that this philosophy and methodology can be learned and used to advantage by anyone who practices leadership, regardless of cultural background and leadership position.

# Introduction
## The Leader's Mental Scorecard

Behind the Leader's Mental Scorecard lies the fact that, as an avid golfer, I have worked a great deal with the psychological side of the game. It is true of all sports that your technical and physical talents limit how far you can go: a good sprinter has a different build than a good mid-distance runner, for example. However, it is true for everyone that the more you practice, the better you get. Whether or not you reach your peak performance – and how often you exploit your full potential – is simply a question of your attitude, which has to do with, among other things, your ability to make optimal decisions, to make a comeback, and to perform under pressure. For many reasons, the psychological element plays a greater role in golf than in any other sport, regardless of the level at which the golfer plays. The performance of an ordinary golfer is just as dependent on psychological factors as it is for the world's best players.

After having studied both professional and ordinary amateur golfers, I realized that the single most important factor for a golfer's level of performance is the ability to adjust strategy and playing style to fit the situation. This ability seems to be almost completely lacking in a great many golfers. Most golfers simply play the way they play: they almost always choose the same approach, no matter what their situation and regardless of whether or not their approach is appropriate to the situation at hand. The funny thing is that many managers do the same thing.

Golf is a game in which you try to hit a ball so that it follows a specially designed course about 6000 meters long, and you try to do this hitting the ball the fewest possible number of times. Part of the logic is, then, to try to hit the ball so it goes far. However, what you see is that many golfers who, in their effort to hit the ball a long way, are willing to give up on hitting the ball so it goes straight. It's kind of in your blood: far is best. And when you end up hitting a ball far into the woods, you try to correct the situation by hitting the ball even harder on your next stroke, often with the result that you hit it even further into the woods. This makes it look as though, more than any other group, golfers seem to live up to Einstein's definition of madness:

The Leader's Mental Scorecard. © Finn Havaleschka.

True insanity is…
Using the same behavior and expecting different results.

However, this is not only true of golfers. Results-oriented managers who make great demands on themselves and their subordinates aim high and run fast, and they demand the same from those around them. But if their ambitions are not realized and there are obstacles, their reaction is almost always to push themselves and others to run even faster. Instead of hitting the ball harder, like golfers, their natural reaction is to invest more resources and demand even more of themselves and their coworkers.

As in all other areas of life, the solutions we choose are a result of our temperament and personality. Cautious players play cautiously. Impatient, risk-taking players take chances. Players with a creative temperament experiment their way through a game, finding new ways to hit the ball, and extroverted players chat with others in order to find the inner composure to play the game. The exact same thing applies to leaders. Another thing is, if you know what kind of personality someone has, it's easy to predict the solution he or she will choose, almost no matter what the situation is – and, almost as importantly, what solutions he or she will *not* choose. Cautious players, just like cautious leaders, would rather not take any chances. They are reluctant to choose risky solutions, no matter how appropriate it may be in the given situation. On the other hand, players willing to take risks choose "safe" solutions only if they feel forced to do so. In the same way, people with a creative temperament are often blind to the traditional solution, and extroverts are often, even when the situation calls for it, unable to look inwards to find the composure necessary to concentrate on what is important, and to do so independently of their social surroundings.

The difference between people who most often utilize their full potential and those who only occasionally do their best is that the first group is good at adapting their problem-solving to the situation at hand, and they are better at selecting a solution that they are fairly well qualified to carry out. This indicates that they have a realistic view of their own abilities and skills, and there we have it: the formula to follow in the mental training of leaders. Leaders must learn to change their leadership style to suit the situation, i.e. learn to choose a solution that is optimal with respect to the situation at hand instead of simply applying their usual methods determined by their temperament and personality. If you hit a ball far into the woods, and you just can't seem to get your game going right, then the solution is to switch to a strategy that will most likely bring you safely back on the fairway. Among other things, this involves choosing a strategy that you are qualified and able to implement, and thus often choosing a different solution than the one that got you into the woods in the first place.

With managers who are strongly structure- and order-oriented and to whom maintaining control is very important, we have seen in practice that this attitude, these psychological aspects, will be a determining factor in their way of approaching and solving problems, and that this will also affect their leadership decisions. In the same way, impatient leaders who are willing to take risks and believe that speed and results are important will include these elements in their decision-making. As with golfers, the solutions leaders choose are often more a result of their personality than of the situation at hand, and that's why their route to success will be the same as for golfers. Good leaders, just like good golfers, must learn to choose a style – an approach to solving the tasks at hand – that suit the situation. Depending on the situation, they must learn to switch from a risk-taking to a more security-oriented style, from a visionary and creative approach to a more controlling one that focuses more on the details, from a highly social and consensus-oriented style to a decisive and presidential style, and so on. They must also learn to have a more objective view of their own abilities so that they can select strategies that they are able to carry out.

The difference between leaders and golfers is that a golfer's situation does not change independently of the golfer him- or herself: the ball lie where it lies, and the distance to the hole does not change unless the golfer changes it. On the other hand, a leader's situation is constantly shifting. Leaders work with dynamic situations and with people. Basically, good human resources leadership starts with a manager traveling, so to speak, to the place where the employee is with respect to that person's personality, psychology and qualifications. If an employee is security-oriented and needs structure and guidelines, then that is where the leader needs to go. If the employee needs to talk and see him- or herself as part of a group, then that's the approach the leader needs to take. If the employee has a creative and experimenting nature, then that's where the leader needs to go. Or if the employee has an impatient, results-oriented nature, then the leader needs to go where that person is coming from. As a leader, you have to learn that you can't just change people and get them to live up to your own expectations and behavior patterns. Coworkers that are used to living life in the fast lane, taking chances and going right to the edge will only for a very short time accept a dictate to stay in the slow lane, driving slowly but surely while watching fast-track colleagues pass. Inversely, it is difficult to entice employees that feel safe and secure in the slow lane to speed up and move out into the passing lane.

It is a fact that we do not change personality during our adult life. Our life experience may make us a bit more patient and a bit more mellow, but an extrovert will not change into an introvert, and a security-oriented person will not suddenly start taking risks. People who are very impatient may with time become slightly more patient, but they'll still be more impatient than people whose patience is in their nature. And this is absolutely fine, because you don't have to change your nature to achieve better results or become a better leader. The only thing you need is to learn to modify your normal behavior to suit the situation rather than trying to make the situation (including your coworkers and others) to change to suit your behavior. In other words,

> Before you try to change others to suit their behavior to your own, as a start try changing your behavior to suit the behavior of others.

This is where the biggest problem and greatest challenge lies for most managers: meeting subordinates not halfway, but in the psychological place where *they* are rather than making them come to you. The idea is to be able to change style. We often see leaders who base their approach on their own personality, attitudes and knowledge, and then they are surprised when things don't move in the desired direction. Going to the place where others are and basing your approach on the way it is natural for *them* to tackle problems essentially requires mental training on your part. Obviously, your experience and ability to empathize play a substantial role as well. If you used to be on the sales staff yourself before you became sales manager, it's easier for you to understand the members of the sales staff and the conditions they work under, even if you haven't been in the exact same situation before. On the other hand, there are many leaders who are actually pretty bad at going to the place where their subordinates are psychologically, even though the same leaders are experienced and good at empathizing. Experience and empathy are one thing, but the most important thing is to be able to *use* your experience and your ability to empathize. Funnily enough, we often act contrary to what our empathic abilities tell us. Empathy, intuition, your understanding of how another person feels about a certain situation, and your feel for what the situation requires can be very, very clear. For a split second – or even a longer period of time – you can be completely aware of the fact that what you are saying or doing will definitely *not* lead to the desired result, but still you continue your inexpedient behavior instinctively, by reflex. We all know the situation.

> Knowing what's right is one thing.
> Doing the right thing is another.

Subordinates are part of the situation that leaders have to be able to assess and deal with. Another crucial factor is the task at hand, the context that the task is a part of, and what the objective of the task is. Certain tasks lend themselves to a more structured, security-oriented and calculating approach; others are best tackled with a more creative, seeking, learning-by-doing attitude. In some cases, the objective of the task can only be reached if you are successful in putting together a team that works together well and has a clear sense of values and attitudes. In other cases, it is a question of putting everything else aside and just get going, and get results – faster, bigger and better.

Thus, as a leader, you must be able to evaluate where your subordinates are coming from psychologically and what their needs are, and determine the nature and purpose of the task. Then you have to be able to adjust your own behavior and way of dealing with problems so it is optimally suited to the situation, the tasks at hand, and the people you will be working together with to carry out these tasks.

The Leader's Mental Scorecard. © Finn Havaleschka.

To be able to do this, you as a leader must:

1. **Know** yourself, i.e. be aware of your normal style as it is determined by your personality and temperament, and thus be aware of your immediate reaction patterns.
2. **Understand** your effect on others, i.e. be aware of how you are perceived by others.
3. **Become familiar with** each person's style as determined by his or her personality and temperament.
4. **Assess** the task at hand, its objective, and the context within which it appears.
5. And, lastly, be able to make a **realistic assessment** of your own abilities and those of others as they relate to the tasks at hand and the objectives you are attempting to achieve.

The purpose of this book is exactly that: to impart to you some methods and tools so you can learn to lead and act in accordance with the needs of your subordinates and of the situation. You don't have to change your personality. I'm not talking about personal development, just about you learning to modify your behavior in certain situations. Our ambition is simply a modification of your behavior that lasts anywhere from a few minutes to a few hours, but nevertheless a modification that seems to make the difference between successful and less successful leadership. The means to this end is the Focused Leadership model, and the toolbox you use is the Leader's Mental Scorecard, which is based on the fundamental rule that

**All other things being equal, what you do not in advance imagine and add to your psychological world, you will have difficulty carrying out in practice in the real world.**

**On the other hand, the more you think, imagine, or put up on your internal television screen about how you will act in a certain way in certain situations, the greater the chances that you will be able to actually do so in reality.**

Good luck, and enjoy!

# Part One
## The Four Focus Areas of Leadership

# Four different approaches to Leadership

## Starring:

The social, considerate and always comforting Integrator Leader.

The inventive, creative and always optimistic Developer Leader.

The quiet, self controlled and always prepared Baser Leader.

The speedy, goal oriented and always competing Result Leader.

The Leader's Mental Scorecard. © Finn Havaleschka.

# Leadership is about having everything under control, avoiding risk and being guarded against the unexpected

Presenting the Baser Leader

When a Baser leader feels he is in control of life, he is in harmony with himself. This state of feeling happy brings with it the sense that things are in order; the future has been planned and is predictable; you know what you have and give everyone their due.

You draw up budgets for the forward-moving process of life, and are reluctant to make decisions whose consequences you cannot predict. You safeguard yourself against unhappiness by guarding against the unexpected.

The Leader's Mental Scorecard. © Finn Havaleschka.

When things don't go the way you intended and life's unpredictability upsets your plans, you become stressed and feverish.

Feelings of happiness disappear, and questions arise: "Who is to blame? Did I calculate wrong? Is there a detail, a rule I overlooked or something I forgot to check?"

Losing happiness, predictability and security in life is one of the worst things that can happen. So you have to guard yourself against it.

The way you do that is by establishing stronger boundaries, more security, more checking things, more rules, and more thorough and detailed planning.

The Leader's Mental Scorecard. © Finn Havaleschka.

# Leadership is about creating results, avoid losing and having the courage to take a chance

## Presenting the Result Leader

For Results leaders, happiness is being with those that are ahead of the pack. You feel best when there's something at stake. In that state, you are in a restless repose – are only yourself when you are in motion. You set goals: high goals, specific goals.

You motivate, radiate enthusiasm, love competition – the game. It's about the right to make fun of the loser. You push, find smart methods, happy to take a chance, cut a corner. You guard yourself against unhappiness by putting more into it than others do.

The Leader's Mental Scorecard. © Finn Havaleschka.

When things don't go the way you promised and planned, when your ambitions have to be curbed, and other people won't play along with you any more or won't put their heart in it, you are disappointed, angry and perhaps a bit aggressive.

Your feeling of happiness disappears. "We were so close! We made one little mistake, maybe, but if you'd just given it an extra push, we would have done it – we would have reached our goal!"

The Leader's Mental Scorecard. © Finn Havaleschka.

The prospect of losing the right to make fun of the loser, to see the chance of victory and great results slipping through your fingers, is a disappointing and sometimes painful experience.

The drive to reclaim your happiness and overcome obstacles stems from thinking about the game, the praise, attention, excitement, the adrenalin kick. The way to get there is to go that extra mile, be committed and take a chance. Nothing ventured, nothing gained.

The Leader's Mental Scorecard. © Finn Havaleschka.

# eadership is about communication, creating understanding and avoiding disagreements and conflicts

## Presenting the Integrator Leader

© Garuda Research Institute - info@garudahr.com

For Integrator leaders, happiness is helping create a fellowship of like-minded people who stick together, have a nice time, and try to predict and live up to other people's expectations as best they can.

They listen to each other, show consideration towards each other, play down conflicts and conflicts of interest, and try to get everyone to pull in the same direction.

These leaders are comfortable in the role of coach, mentor and person everyone rallies around. They safeguard themselves against unhappiness by avoiding conflict and make unpleasant decisions together.

The Leader's Mental Scorecard. © Finn Havaleschka.

When things don't go as you had hoped, when results fail to materialize, and the group's feeling of fellowship and solidarity disappear, you end up feeling lonely.

Feelings of security and acceptance disappear; people will go their own way, find reasons and scapegoats. "It's hopeless; we lack leadership," they think, but they don't say it aloud.

The Leader's Mental Scorecard. © Finn Havaleschka.

When the sense of fellowship disappears, and dialog is replaced by criticism and barriers, the feeling of acceptance disappears as well. When that happens, you feel pain, and you aren't yourself any more.

You suggest compromises, yield, try to live up to the expectations of others, delegate responsibility and set aside your right and duty to lead. "We simply have to learn to understand each other better; then everything will be good again."

The Leader's Mental Scorecard. © Finn Havaleschka.

# Leadership is about looking forward, creating opportunities and eliminating tightening structures and rules

## Presenting the Developer Leader

For Development leaders, happiness is creating, seeing new opportunities, making changes, seeing the road ahead and showing others the way. The worst things are limitations, a lack of visions, reactionaries, pessimism and conservative inertia.

What drives them is the butterflies-in-the-stomach feeling of happiness when they get an idea and tell everyone about the fantastic opportunities – that no one else spotted. Things are just waiting to be realized. You create the future. Anything is possible. Being forward-looking is the best way to safeguard your self against unhappiness.

The Leader's Mental Scorecard. © Finn Havaleschka.

When ideas go up in smoke and pragmatic critics and the ruthlessness of what can and cannot be done in practice reduce visions to castles in the air, then you have to reluctantly admit that the time was not right for others to recognize your genius.

They didn't understand you because you didn't communicate well enough – you didn't go into enough detail – and because many people prefer to hold onto what they know and stick with the safe choice.

You feel pressured, and the approval and appreciation disappears along with the butterflies. But all is not lost: there must be a way, something you missed.

The Leader's Mental Scorecard. © Finn Havaleschka.

The way back to happiness is creativity and taking the broad outlook, combined with the will to change and reject outdated concepts, rules and limitations. You should and must get other people to see the world in its own light.

It is all about promoting and communicating your new insight. We are no longer looking for a "missing link" –for there is no link. If you want to be a leader, you must be ready to make that quantum leap without being fussy about unimportant details.

The Leader's Mental Scorecard. © Finn Havaleschka.

# I. The Concept of Development
Ideology or Facts

Having introduced our four main characters, it will be quite natural to ask: Is it possible to develop our personality in order for us also to master the type of leadership that does not come natural to us?

Over the past 10-15 years, I have become more and more skeptical about the prospects of realizing the personal development that the development concept of the 1970s and 1980s promised us. In the field of developmental psychology, there is general agreement that

> "the individual human, as it develops towards higher stages of psychological development, shows a higher degree of autonomy and ability to handle stress, greater integration of intellect and feelings, stronger human and moral values and awareness, and a less self-centered perception and interaction with other people°.[10]

Basically, I am now convinced that the developmental paradigm that has shaped the developmental activities we have carried out over the past 20 years is based more on ideology and hopeful thinking than fact. If I am right it has an important bearing on all future projects within the HRM&D area. We need to be less ambitious and change the methods - like in the direction that I am suggesting in this book.

---

[10] Harald Harung, Dennis Heaton and Charles Alexander, "A Unified Theory of Leadership: experiences of higher states of consciousness in world-class leaders"; Leadership and Organization Development Journal Vol. 16, No. 7, 1996, 47. (MCB University Press, Bradford, UK). For a more in-depth discussion of this developmental paradigm, see Robert Kegan, In Over Our Heads: The Mental Demands of Modern Life (Cambridge, MA: Harvard University Press, 1994); Jane Loevinger, Ego Development: Conceptions and Theories (New York: Van Nostrand Reinhold, 1976); and Abraham Maslow, Toward a Psychology of Being (New York: Van Nostrand Reinhold, 1968).

**I will explain my opinion in the following. If you are not especially inte-
rested in this problem complex, please feel free to skip the following and
go directly to the next chapter, page 49. Whether or not you share my opinion in this matter has no bearing on what you will get out of your work
with the Mental Scorecard.**

Generally, the developmental concept I quoted above speaks of development
at two levels. At one level, or in one of the dimensions, there is said to be a
development in morals, values and ethics, i.e. development toward a greater
degree of capability in caring, empathy, personal integrity, openness, trust,
etc. In other words, it is a development in the way we treat each other, moving towards a more love-thy-neighbor type of behavior. I'm not saying that
personal development like that cannot take place, or that it isn't development
that we should strive for: I'm simply saying that I have yet to see proof from
practicing developmental psychologists, psychological researchers or others
that such development has been observed – at least as a general human phen-
omenon.

An illustration of the truth value of this contention of mine is a few re-
forms that were worded by a Sumerian king almost 5000 years ago. Zecharia
Sitchin, an authority in translation of the Sumerian tablets, tells us:

> *The reform decree of Urukagina [the ruler] listed the evils of his
> time first, then the reforms. The evils he wanted to eliminate
> consisted primarily of the unfair use by supervisors of their
> powers to take the best for themselves; the abuse of official
> status; the extortion of high prices by monopolistic groups....
> The rights of the blind, poor, widowed, and orphaned were
> reinstated. A divorced woman – nearly 5,000 years ago – was
> granted the protection of the law.*[11]

Apparently, there's nothing new under the sun. There is nothing in our re-
corded history to indicate that humanity has improved its human and moral
values, much less become less self-centered.

The other dimension in this developmental concept is the development
in individual personality traits that are mapped and identified in and by so-

---

[11]  Zecharia Sitchin, The Twelfth Planet (Santa Fe, NM: Bear & Company: 1991), 48-49.

called "trait theories". In trait theories, it is a person's personality traits that express themselves in a need for order, structure, security, need for information on and control of details, influence, independence, performance, social contact, etc., and the behavior derives from these traits. I know of no theories or research results that state how these two levels are connected, i.e. how the claims of developmental psychology can be integrated with trait theory and how this can be expressed both developmentally and behaviorally.[12]

One approach to clarifying the issue could be to go back to the question that has always occupied mankind: to what extent the various personality traits identified by trait theorists are a consequence of genetic and biological factors or social factors rooted in a person's upbringing. In other words, is a person's need for order, for example, a consequence of his genetic heritage, or is it a consequence of the environment he grew up in and the influences he was exposed to in that environment? One point of view is that people's individual personality traits exist and develop as they do because they played (and perhaps still play) a crucial role in human evolution, a process in which the fight to survive resulted in the development of certain traits and thus behavior that ensured the survival of the species. Another point of view is that the degree to which a person needs order, for example, is a result of the way that person was brought up. Eysenck, one of the fathers of trait theory and also spokesman for the evolution viewpoint, says *"personality theories that are not in accordance with the newer evolution theories have very little chance of being right."*[13] In 1982, this same Eysenck expressed the view that genetic factors could explain two-thirds of the variance in the personality traits identified: in other words, why the behavior of some people is dominated by certain traits to a higher degree than others. Whether it is two-thirds or more or less than two-thirds has been debated ever since, but as research into our genes gives us more and more knowledge about the influence of our genes on our physical functions, intellectual abilities and mental-emotional states, everyone agrees that biological factors play a sizeable role.[14] Eysenck was also of the opinion that it is this trait variance in people that has ensured

---

[12] Read more about trait theory in Lawrence A. Pervin, Daniel Cervone, and Oliver P. John, Personality: Theory and Research (New York, NY: John Wiley & Sons, Inc., 1997), 225-296, and Edward J. Murray, Motivation and Emotion. (Prentice-Hall, Inc. New Jersey, 1964).

[13] Pervin, 239. May I add that there are other opinions in this debate that it would take too long to go into here.

[14] Pervin, 271.

the survival of the species. In other words, it is good for the survival of the species that some people have a greater need for order, for example, than others.

One example of the results of research into the connection between genetics/biology and personality traits is that certain people produce more adrenaline than others, and this is reflected in how they score on the performance and competition trait in personality testing. The genetic explanation is that women's bodies do not generally produce the same amount of testosterone and adrenaline (epinephrine) as men's do. On chromosome 10 there is a gene called CYP17 that produces an enzyme that allows the body to convert cholesterol into testosterone, epinephrine and other substances. We know that testosterone has something to do with the development of gender and muscles and that two different versions of adrenaline help the body prepare for fight or flight.[15]

One example of the significance of this gene is illustrated by an American researcher's study of the production of testosterone in female and male athletes: in this case, two men's and two women's basketball teams. The men's daily average testosterone level was a good deal higher than that of the female players, which simply confirms what we know about the difference in the testosterone/estrogen balance between the two sexes. However, this researcher tested the testosterone levels of all the players immediately before a game. It turned out that the testosterone levels in the male players had increased fourfold, whereas there was only a slight increase in the female players. The players were all tested again right after their games. The men that won their game had even higher testosterone levels, but the men who lost theirs had levels that had dropped to below the normal daily level. Men get a high from winning, a fact that most of us men know well. It is a fantastic feeling that biology has partly barred most women from experiencing, for better or for worse: There was no difference in the women's levels: Whether they were on the winning or losing team, the level of testosterone their bodies produced fell to their usual daily levels right after the game. This explains why many men become elated when their favorite team wins and, if they lose, men become silent, negative, depressed – or perhaps even violent. No

---

[15]  Matt Ridley, Genome: The Autobiography of a Species in 23 Chapters (New York, NY: HarperCollins, 1999).

one doubts the fact that the difference in the reactions of the two genders is biologically determined far more than it is environmentally determined.[16]

An analysis of developments over the past 20 years in some of the personality traits that the trait theorists work with clearly shows that there have been no changes. My own scoring of 16 personality traits ranging from system flexibility and need for order to empathy and confidence and again to psychological robustness and the need to perform is today exactly the same as it was when I measured it for the first time in 1982. So, over the past 20 years, we have not become more flexible, willing to take risks, willing to change, empathic, or trusting; nor have we any less need for limits, structure, details, rules, or security, or thus any less need for the predictability that "apparently" lies behind this behavior.[17] On the other hand, a t-test measuring the difference between the normal distribution in the scores for 14,905 men and 7,146 women showed that there is a significant difference between the two sexes in all personality traits except for the need for freedom. The t-test shows that the difference in the scores does not have its origins in statistical coincidence, but can be traced back to the characteristics in the two groups. The biggest differences turned out to be in personality traits such as competitiveness, influence, self-confidence, and psychological robustness, differences that are in complete concord with the different genetic backgrounds for the production of testosterone and estrogen in the two genders.

In a number of examples taken from biogenetic research, Professor Helmuth Nyborg, Institute of Psychology, University of Aarhus, clearly showed that these differences can be attributed to differences in childhood environment and upbringing to a limited extent only.[18] One of Nyborg's examples dealt with the consequences of treating a group of infertile men, as experts at the Middlesex Hospital in London did. The men were infertile because they were unable to produce sperm cells. They had reduced gonad function: a failure to secrete the most important sex hormones, a process which is controlled by the pituitary gland. By inserting an automatic pump in the body, it was possible to stimulate the production of these sex hor-

---

[16] I have this example in some of my teaching materials: a copy from a book, unfortunately without any indication of source. I hope you can believe and forgive me anyway.

[17] Finn Havaleschka, Where did the Development go? (Risskov, Denmark: Garuda Research Institute, 2002). Can be downloaded from www.garudahr.com.

[18] Helmuth Nyborg, Køn, Hormoner og Samfund (Copenhagen, Denmark: Dansk Psykologisk Forlag, 1997).

mones, and this sparked off the formation of sperm cells. For most of the men and their wives, everything went well. The men became fertile and able to fertilize. However, the treatment also had some unintended side effects. Shortly afterwards, about half the couples were in the throes of divorce.

> Upon closer examination of their relationships, it became clear that the wives were becoming more and more anxious and worried about a radical change in their husband's personality as treatment continued. Before the treatment began, many of the men were apparently somewhat shy and introverted. ….such introverted personality traits would characterize a man whose androgen levels are low.[19]

According to the principle (of optimal levels of androgen), the men should have begun to act aggressively as a function of the androgen treatment.

> And the men in treatment certainly did that! Several of the men actually took over command of their relationship with their spouses, and one of them even began to physically abuse his wife. Some got into bar fights or street fights, and in extreme cases, their markedly changed behavior brought them into contact with the police. The behavioral changes can be explained by the relationship between the brain's behavioral control center and the level of androgen in the blood.[20]

What is upbringing and what is biological and genetic? From both trait theory and practice, we know that the combination of the traits introvertedness and submissiveness are characteristic of people who are exactly that: submissive, quiet and introverted. There are people who accept being under the control of others to a great extent and who seldom stand up and say yes or no. They are reactive and passive rather than proactive and controlling.

In this connection, I can't help thinking about all the development projects I was involved in back in the 1980s and the beginning of the 1990s, projects whose purpose was to create more employee empowerment, i.e. de-

---

[19] Nyborg, 107-108.
[20] Nyborg, 108.

velop a greater will in employees to take responsibility and make decisions independently.

The purpose of the development mantra of the 1980s – "It's easier to get forgiveness than permission" – was exactly to inspire workers to become more proactive. So, management told them again and again: *If you are in doubt, then do what you think is most appropriate, and if it turns out that it wasn't quite so appropriate, then count on being forgiven.* When we didn't see any major overall changes as a result of this slogan and development activities derived from it, it could well be because this behavior is more genetic than it is a result of upbringing and environment. The fact was that if we did experience change in the desired direction, it was short-term change. We saw just as often that people did not want change, so they defended their existing position.

A little jokingly and a little seriously, I put it to you to consider the following questions. Does a person become introverted and submissive because while he was growing up he was bullied and his personality was repressed, or was he bullied and repressed because he was introverted and submissive due to the fact that his body produced low levels of androgen? And how much can he move himself away from this behavior in the direction of more proactive, involved and empowered behavior without hormonal supplements and simply as a result of positive psychological, educational and behavioral stimuli? As you can imagine, doubt has begun to creep into my mind.

This does not mean that it is okay to bully and keep other people down. It simply means that some people are more predisposed towards proactive, involved and participatory behavior, and it is difficult to get people who are *not* that way to adopt those behavioral patterns – at least in the form of a lasting change in their behavior.

Another personality trait that can apparently also – at least partly – be explained genetically, is the qualities and behavior that express themselves in empathy, understanding and taking care of other people. The first of the genes that have something to do with this were found in 1977; they are responsible for the transport of the substance serotonin around in our bodies. It turns out that this gene does not function in autistic people.

The reason why that is relevant is that autistic people do not perceive and understand things on an emotional level.

The next step was the discovery of a connection between the function of this gene, the production of the substance serotonin, and the small part of the brain called the amygdala, which is a group of neurons in our limbic system that has something to do with our emotional behavior. It also receives signals from the eyes, ears and nose, *"and seems to carry out some sort of low-level automatic computation on these signals – important in the functioning of the social brain."*[21] Much seems to indicate that this part of the brain, this lump of neurons, is generally larger in women than in men. So, as a starting point, the trait of social empathy and thus the ability to perceive or register other people's emotional states and reactions seems to be genetically determined.[22] Perhaps that is why women are generally better at showing and practicing solicitious behavior than men. This probably doesn't mean that people with low empathy (low serotonin levels) cannot be or cannot learn to be more considerate; it simply means that we are predisposed to exhibiting this type of behavior to different degrees. The consequences of this discovery with respect to our expectations to personal development and the psychological methods of education we have employed up until now – in the belief that it worked – are illustrated by the changes that have been made in the treatment of autism. Therapeutic treatment has been replaced by cognitive behavioral modification therapy. For example, the patients are shown pictures of people in different emotional states. The patients then learn, in a purely intellectual processing process, which feelings each of the pictures represents and how it is most appropriate for them to react to people in that emotional state.

Another example is the fact that too little dopamine in the brain is the cause of indecision. The greater the lack of dopamine, the more this indecision moves from being ordinary indecision to a lacking ability to initiate conscious physical movements. In its extreme form, a lack of dopamine results in Parkinson's disease. The gene that initiates production of dopamine is found in chromosome number 11 and is called D4DR.[23] Thus there are indications that this gene has an influence on the variance in people's energy level and motor capacity.

A last example is a hormone called oxytocin, which is made in the hypothalamus and whose function in relation to child labor and breast feeding

---

[21] Jack Challoner, The Brain (London: Macmillan Publishers Ltd, 2000), 36.
[22] Challoner, 17-49.
[23] Ridley, 161-172.

have been now for many years. Though, not until fairly recently, scientist have discovered that the hormone is also related to a number of mental states and associated behaviour. So far, scientists have only found the gene that triggers the production of this hormone in a certain strain of mice. The corresponding gene has yet to be found in humans, but researchers are certain that the production of this hormone is triggered by a gene in humans as well. This hormone seems to play many roles, but its main function seems to be connected with feelings of security, openness, solicitude – and curiosity as well. On a physical level, the production of this hormone is associated with a woman's ability to produce breast milk and the desire or need to nurse her newborn baby. It is generally true that this desire or need and thus a woman's emotional connection with her baby increases when her body produces more oxytocin. Strangely, however, this bonding function between mother and child is not gender-specific or unilaterally determined by the mother. It turns out that babies also produce this hormone, a production that is triggered by suckling, regardless of the baby's gender.

In addition, it turns out that also men (of all ages) produce this hormone. Experiments with rats show that if you give them low doses of oxytocin, they become less fearful and more curious. *"They are more likely to dare to leave the safety of the nest and explore unfamiliar surroundings. Oxytocin has a clear antianxiety effect."*[24] Other interesting connections between this hormone and behavior are that the presence of this substance in rats augments their ability to remember, strengthens the attachments between them, increases their calm/relaxation, reduces the feeling of physical pain, and boosts their learning capacity. Everything points to this substance having the same effect on people. Knowing full well that it has not yet been scientifically proven, I believe there is much to indicate it is no coincidence that some people are more open, trusting and curious than others; that people fall in love and that some people fall in love more easily and often than others; or that a special mother-child bond exists, a bond that is generally far stronger than the father-child relationship. This again indicates that the quality and nature of the relationships people form with each other is far from being determined by upbringing and socialization alone.

---

[24] Kerstin U. Moberg, The Oxytocin Factor (Cambridge, MA: Da Capo Press, 2003), 66.

INSEAD Professor Manfred F.R. Kets de Vries, psychoanalyst and executive coach, says, *"People cannot change their personality, but they can change their behavior."*[25] My own experience has been the same as that of Professor Kets de Vries. Not much indicates that we can change people's need for details or security, their dependency on the rules and structures that give them a sense of security, their ability to empathize and the degree to which they are self-centered, make independent decisions, etc.

Personality seems to be a very constant element with respect to the actual behavior it engenders, the needs people try to satisfy, and the values people strive to realize in their actual behavior. All in all, it takes me in the direction of more realistic ambitions as far as personal development is concerned. We should, of course, try to protect our fellow man and the environment we live in and make our living from, but to change a person from being basically security-oriented to basically risk-taking, from driving in the slow lane to driving in the fast lane, or from being a controlling leader to being a leader who delegates – I don't believe anymore that it can be done. However, I do believe that we can learn to be better at adapting our behavior to the situation so that we become, for example, less controlling and more delegating in certain situations, or the other way around for shorter periods of time.

---

[25]  Danish periodical Ledelse I Dag ("Leadership Today") 57, 2004), 26-30.

# II. Mental Training
## Basic Principles

In the world of sports, the importance of psychological factors in achieving results has been discussed to an increasing extent for several years. It is the psychological aspect, the mental aspect, that makes the difference. But what is mental training, really? We might have an idea of what it is, perhaps, but what is it really that these sports psychologists do? Do they have some kind of knowledge or insight, some key to the depths of our psychological makeup that can help us combat nervousness, dampen our arrogance or fear of **failure**, and instead call forth our ability to be at peace with ourselves, in equilibrium, fully self-confident, and deeply concentrated on what we are doing, using our skills, competences, knowledge, potential to the full?

Or is the winner mentality (both of athletes and of leaders) that shows itself in, among other things, no fear of failure and a well-developed self-confidence, staying calm and balanced a gift we are born with? More and more research seems to indicate this is the case. Sports psychologists, ordinary psychologists, and therapists – none of them can change your personality. At best, they can help you modify your behavior and act a little differently in certain situations than you otherwise would have done. And that is precisely the purpose of mental training. There's nothing mystical about it and no hidden secrets in mental training.

To put it briefly, you could say that the aim of mental training – for leaders as well as athletes – is to develop your ability to make conscious choices. Making conscious choices means you are not only very aware of what you're choosing; you are also aware of what you are *not* choosing. Let me give you a couple of example cases in which I am convinced mental training could have helped make for better leadership.

Once, many years ago, I was given the classic choice of either resigning or being fired. The problem wasn't my lack of professional skills or ability. No, I was given this choice because my boss and I had different personalities and different temperaments, and this meant that we focused on different things. My focus was on results, getting ahead and creating something. His focus was on structure, on whether what I was doing was within my area of responsibility, and whether the suggestions I made were within the given rules and customs. This meant that our attempts at communication missed and finally failed completely. I believe my attitude was that I got results and that should be enough. I could certainly see where his focus was, but I didn't have the ability to see things from his point of view. Intellectually, I knew where he was coming from, but I couldn't mentally go there myself. It seemed unnecessary to me to take my starting point where he wanted me to; it seemed to restrictive, too silly – a waste of time. And he had the same problem. He could not mentally go to the place where I was coming from. I am certain that if we'd had a common language and a shared map of the world to look at, we would both have acted differently than we did.

We were each very much aware of where we ourselves were coming from: what motivated our behavior, ambitions and goals. Each of us also had a pretty good idea of where the other person was coming from, too, but we were completely unable to go to each others' "place" and start a discussion there, on the other person's terms.

We all know of examples like this. Here is another one. Once I worked as a consultant for a fairly large group of companies. The group CEO was (and is still) incredibly goal-oriented, impatient and creative. Things that in the world inside his head should be possible to accomplish in a single year took two or three years to do in the real world, so it didn't take long for him to be way ahead of the rest of the organization. He was always way out in front, both in his mind and his actions. It wasn't in his nature to wait for others, so he wasn't very good at it, nor was he skilled at obtaining the understanding and acceptance of others in order to create a shared platform for decisions and their implementation. We discussed this problem often. Intellectually, he had no trouble understanding that he needed to hold back and not move forward so quickly, but he was unable to transform his understanding on a psychological level and thus also unable to put it into practice. In the end, it cost him his job.

Looking back, it is easy to find situations from managerial life – and in all other parts of life – when a lack of ability to go to a different place mentally creates obstacles and conflicts, in spite of all kinds of good intentions. However, there are good examples, too.

Once, back when I worked at Bang & Olufsen at their headquarters in

Struer, Denmark, I went to a meeting in the IT and Financial department. There was a great deal of dissatisfaction among the employees about various working conditions and decisions that had been made, and now they were holding a meeting at which the department head would try to straighten things out. The department head must have been 27-28 years old at the time. In spite of his young age, he tackled the situation extremely well. Everyone left the meeting with an excellent understanding of the situation, and they were satisfied and motivated to take on their share of the work to be done.

What that young man did was a masterpiece of leadership. He listened, he understood, he explained so people could understand, he showed consideration, he gave people individual attention, and he had a clear vision of where the company's activities were taking us and what the necessary processes were. In spite of the harsh tone he was met with at the beginning, at no time did he take it personally, feel insulted, or try to defend himself. He explained, clarified things and listened to people's good ideas. The people at the meeting became involved in the process, and it became their project. That young leader has since enjoyed an excellent career: his name is Thorleif Krarup, and today he is one of Denmark's most prominent business leaders.

As you will note from the above, Krarup started out by explaining, showing consideration, and giving people individual attention. At this point, his focus was on the individual worker and his or her perception and understanding of the situation. Next, he focused on and explained the vision, purpose and idea behind the changes that were to be implemented. Then he described the financial and time aspects, made suggestions and came up with ideas for activity plans, etc. Openly and effortlessly, he changed focus to suit the needs of his coworkers and the situation. He found and began his leadership at the place where his subordinates were coming from. He made mental shifts from one moment to the next. For him it was/is natural, I believe, because he is a man so much in balance with himself that he has no trouble moving from one place to the next. We others have to practice in order to be able to do it.

It is here, on the psychological level, that we can make the greatest gain with the least amount of effort. I contend that the unconscious mixing of different types or qualities of leadership are why the great majority of less effectual leadership situations arise. A deliberate focus, deep concentration, and reaching the mental state where we make the right decisions, find ourselves and create harmony – this all happens when we become aware of the factors that control our behavior and the choices we make. Not until we become aware of this can we make a conscious choice to move away from one area of focus to another, depending on what the situation dictates, instead of reacting as dictated by our personality, instinctive reactions and force of habit.

You cannot change your personality, but you can learn to modify your behavior and make different choices than you usually make for a short or longer period of time. You are your personality; you can't run from that. At most, you can modify it short-term.

Look at it in the following way. Your consciousness is like a spotlight shining its light out onto a landscape: a sharply delineated cone of light resting for moments at a time on different situations, events, words and thought sequences. Often you don't actually become aware of a situation in any kind of detail before the spotlight moves on, throwing its light onto a different part of the landscape. The spotlight is constantly moving, erratically and at changing speeds, as if it has a life of its own. Your consciousness does not always have time to focus, to note the details. In these situations, we act in a state of lack of awareness. It's our personality that controls it; we leave it to habit, routine or instinct to determine what we do and how we react. It's a bit like driving in a car. We just drive. We don't think about how it works, and only if something unusual happens do we notice it at all. Our reactions and routines are already coded in.

In most cases, we are not the ones controlling where the spotlight goes. I contend that when we act as leaders, we often do so in a mental state of absence of awareness, a state that is the biggest obstacle to your ability to develop your leadership competencies. Being conscious of what you are focusing on is thus also where the foundation for developing yourself as a leader lies. In the following, I will introduce to you a model that can help you become familiar with and recognize what it is the spotlight is shining on so that you can consciously decide to either stop the spotlight moving to take a closer look at things or to move the spotlight so that it shines onto other areas and you can seek other solutions. I believe that if the spotlight (your awareness) shines on something that you have never seen before or have only met in passing, then your chances of recognizing what the spotlight is shining on are quite small, which means that you won't be able to make conscious choices, either, on the basis of such fleeting recognition.

In other cases, you can definitely recognize the situation, e.g. if the person before you feels hurt. Intuitively, there are little flashes of awareness that tell you why, and you get a sense of how it feels as well, but you feel and register this only a fleeting moment because the spotlight, your awareness, has already moved on to something else, a place that is about something completely different. Maybe this is because a little voice inside you says, "Forget it. Move the spotlight. I can't do anything about it anyway." In other words, because there is an absence of awareness on your part, you suppress your observation and your feelings, and (perhaps) also cut yourself off from courses of action that are more appropriate than your usual ones.

What will make you stop and consciously find and analyze the alternatives to your usual behavioral choices, the ones that your personality determines, is the Focus Model. In chapter III, I will give you a thorough introduction to the model and how you can use the model to help you make conscious choices and become a better leader. In order to see and put the following mental training principle into perspective, here follows a short introduction to the model.

I divide leadership, leadership behavior and leadership situations up into four areas: One area for Baser leadership[26], one for Results leadership, one for Integrator leadership, and one for Development leadership (see Figure 1).

---

[26] This is a self made term. Find definition on the following pages.

## Figure 1. Model for Focused Leadership

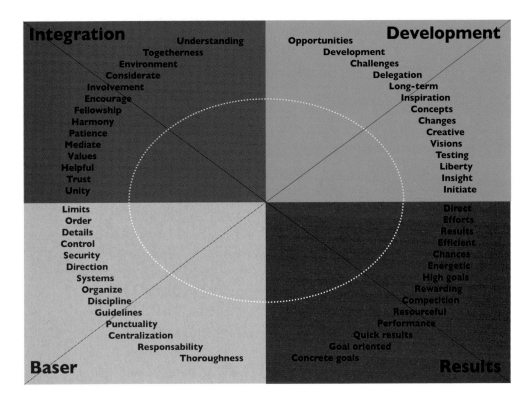

The key words in each of the four areas, or fields, of the model generally describe the qualities in the leadership, personality, leadership style and leadership areas that we meet and deal with on an everyday basis. I will now give you a short introduction to each of these four fields. One of these areas we call the Baser field (see Figure 2).

## Figure 2. The Baser field

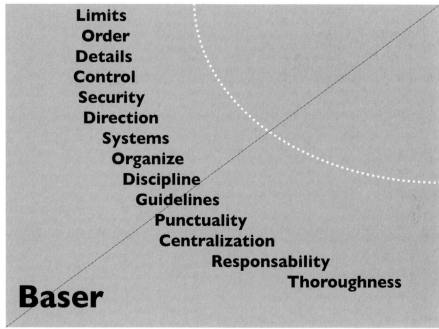

Limits
Order
Details
Control
Security
Direction
Systems
Organize
Discipline
Guidelines
Punctuality
Centralization
Responsability
Thoroughness

**Baser**

*See the presentation of the Baser Leader in the illustrations pages 23 - 26.*

In this field, the focus (or the spotlight) is on order, systematicism, limits, structures, security, details, and creating predictability by making and following plans, organizing, calculating and controlling. Baser leadership is about all the basics that have to be agreed on and in place when you want people to work together towards a shared goal. At the same time, it's obvious that there are some people, both leaders and subordinates, who have a far greater focus on this field or type of task and a far greater talent for doing this kind of work that others, and they have this by virtue of their personality, temperament, preferences, or what motivates them. Some people's spotlights are permanently focused on the Baser area. It's where they feel at home and secure, and they feel safe there because they're doing something they are good at.

This was the area my former boss had his spotlight focused on. It was what he was good at, and it was what I felt was simply something that kept us from moving ahead. This is also the area the group CEO I referred to above did not focus on: not because it was his job to plan and implement that type of activity, but because he should have allowed other people the time and the room to do it.

Moving counterclockwise, I call the next area in the model the Results field. This is where the focus is on achieving actual results. People with their spotlight shining on this area put pressure on others, push, take chances, exploit the situation of the moment, are impatient, get straight to the point and sometimes go over the line. They work in the short term, with the attitude that things have to be done right now. See Figure 3. Again, there are lots of tasks in an organization that can be identified if we shine the spotlight into the Results field. Results tasks aren't just to be found in the sales and production functions. They can be found all over the organization: in maintenance, development, administration and other areas. There's always something you just have to finish before you can move onto something else. The tasks you have to complete before you can go do something else are Results tasks.

## Figure 3. The Result field

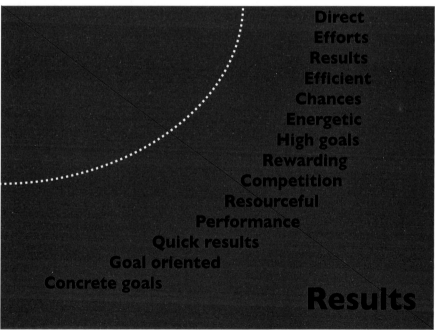

*See the presentation of the Result Leader in the illustrations page 27 - 30.*

The Leader's Mental Scorecard. © Finn Havaleschka.

There are also people who primarily have their spotlight set on the Results field and thus primarily focus and work on this type of task. This was the area I felt that my boss back then did not have any focus on at all. The way it looked to me, everything else came first for him – and not until everything else was done could we even think about taking chances and just going for something. For him, the basic things were apparently never quite done, and I didn't have the patience to wait.

Continuing up to the next field, the third area the spotlight hits is the Integrator field. The focus here is on interaction between people, avoiding conflicts, creating consensus, getting others to go along, and getting others to understand. People with their spotlights on this area learn what other people's expectations are and try their best to understand and live up to them. No matter where we are, if there is more than one person in the room, then there will be a need for a spotlight shining on the blue field to a greater or lesser extent, not just for a few seconds, but for longer periods of time. The need for harmony, understanding, acceptance, love and trust combined with different interests, different values, different goals, different personalities and different temperaments make Integrator leadership and Integrator activities a permanent and essential part of everyday life. For some people, this focus and this type of activity is a natural extension of their personality. Thorleif Krarup mastered this area of leadership: "He listened, he understood, he explained things so you could understand them, he was considerate of everyone and gave everyone individual attention." See Figure 4.

## Figure 4. The Integrator field

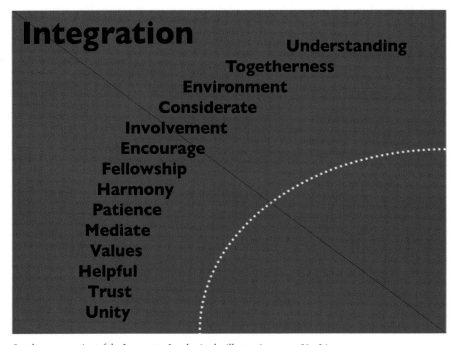

# Integration

Understanding
Togetherness
Environment
Considerate
Involvement
Encourage
Fellowship
Harmony
Patience
Mediate
Values
Helpful
Trust
Unity

*See the presentation of the Integrator Leader in the illustrations page 31 - 34.*

Even a quick glance at the key words in Figure 4 make it clear that neither my former boss, the group CEO I told you about earlier, nor I had our spotlights trained on this area to any great extent. It's not that we don't understand, intellectually, that there is a need for this type of leadership, focus and attitude, generally as well as in specific situations. For us, however, the spotlight doesn't shine on this area for very long at a time. We understand and sense, intuitively in a few flashes here and there, that a person needs help, trust, understanding, and sympathy, but then the spotlight moves on, quickly, after a split second, over to the area that is natural for us. The fourth and last area is what I call the Development field. People focused on this area are busy thinking up and formulating concepts, values and visions. They take the longer view, experiment with new thoughts and ideas, and seek a greater understanding of backgrounds, contexts and correlations (see Figure 5). As is the case with the other three areas, this field can be seen from a tasks-oriented or a personality-oriented point of view. Working with the development of concepts, ideas, and visions and working on tasks that require creativity, insight and overview is the foundation of the development of any organization and – on a different scale – a prerequisite for the development of any function and new ways to carry out tasks and solve problems regardless of organizational location and hierarchical level. This was the area the above-mentioned CEO was focused on. His mental spotlight kept his awareness permanently focused on the green field – and this laid the foundation for the "absence" of awareness of the other three areas. The same thing happens to most of us every day.

## Figure 5. The Development field

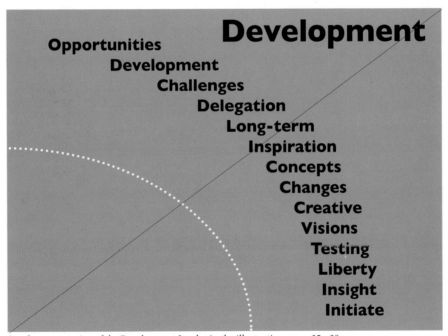

*See the presentation of the Development Leader in the illustrations page 35 - 39.*

This is where mental training comes into the picture. As I said above, you don't have to change your personality; you simply have to learn to change your behavior for short moments in certain situations and sequences of events.

Focused Leadership is about learning to sit in the middle, so to speak, and from this position consciously allow our spotlight of awareness to seek alternatives to our usual preferences. And, in reality, that's not so hard to do.

Once you have the awareness, the rest is a question of giving yourself a sufficient degree of mental and emotional freedom to want to see, dare to see, and shine that spotlight into one of the other fields, as illustrated in Figure 6.

## Figure 6. Focused Leadership

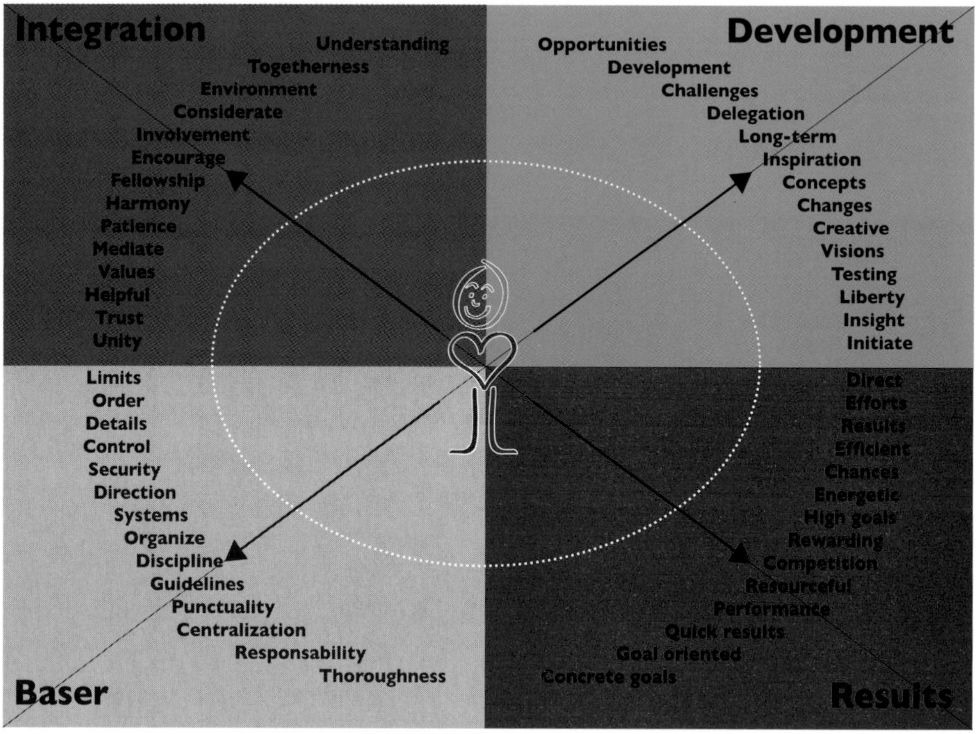

## Your Coworker's Personality

One thing, however, is having gained an awareness of the four fields and developing an ability to move around in them, and thus in certain situations releasing yourself from the behavior determined by your personality. The next thing is to use this ability to go to the places where other people are or are coming from. It is, of course, also true of your subordinates that their focus and the way they perceive and learn things is also determined by their personality and temperament. So if, as leaders, we want to develop and lead other people, then we have to take our starting point in each person's "normal" method of solving problems – and thus their learning style – and adapt what we want them to learn and adapt our leadership style to their style.

The Leader's Mental Scorecard. © Finn Havaleschka.

Imagine a teacher that has four students: Thomas, a creative and experimental soul; Peter – sensitive, poetic and talkative; Mike, who always tackles things head-on; and Larry, who is systematic and borderline pedantic. If the teacher uses the same teaching method with these four students, the probability is that none of them will get the optimal result out of the process. Presumably, it is obvious to most of us that, if the four students are learn most effectively, the teacher should choose a method of instruction that best suits their temperament and personalities. Being an effective leader or teacher means you have to be able to adjust your leadership style and teaching methods to the individual person.

Our school system is beginning to realize that different children learn in different ways, so teaching should be adapted to the differences rather than the similarities. Ideally, this has always been a requirement in leadership. Leaders must learn to differentiate their teaching methods to suit the differences between their students rather than their similarities. But before you can do this, you have to get to know yourself and become aware of not just what you choose to focus on, but also what you choose *not* to focus on. To lead others, you must learn where these other people are, i.e. which of the four fields does their spotlight shine on more or less permanently. Mostly, it's enough to use the key words in the model. If you can identify the words that best describe a coworker of yours, then it is easy to get to the core of their personality, temperament and the motives that drive them, and thus go where they are, to the place they're coming from. Then the next step is to find out the effect you have on others, i.e. how others see you, so you don't blindly believe that everyone understands you on your own terms. Once these things are in place, it is a question of a conscious will to find the courage to move away from the known, safe and secure focus area your personality puts you in. This is where the next tool in the toolbox comes into the picture. I call it the Leader's Mental Scorecard, and it contains a number of examples of leadership actions you must practice both mentally and in actuality so that you can learn to consciously and easily move from one field to another.

**Thus you could say that Focused Leadership is a way to lead; but it also includes a form of mental training, an approach to leading others whose purpose is to develop your ability to make conscious leadership choices.**

The Leader's Mental Scorecard. © Finn Havaleschka.

Just how you do this, I'll get to in the second part of the book. First, though, I would like to offer some more general existential reflections that I hope will make it easier for you to master Focused Leadership. I believe that whether or not you allow yourself enough mental and emotional freedom to exploit your entire potential and consciously move from one area to another, and thus see and learn about the qualities that are represented by the individual areas[26], in the end, it depends on your basic philosophy of life, i.e. what you see as being the purpose of your existence and the moral and ethical framework you build up around how you live your life. Solemn? Deep? Yes, perhaps, but you need to have a good, close look at yourself if you want to go forward from here.

## Self-Actualization

Do you know that state of being wholly concentrated on what you are doing? You've shut everything else out. Things flow. You are yourself, separated from your surroundings yet part of them, integrated in and a part of what you are doing. You can't separate things. Everything is connected and takes place in a harmonic progression. You have no sense of time. You are just happy: wholly yourself, in tune with your own nature. That is the condition we sometimes find ourselves in when we complete a task, paint, write, tend to our flowers, play golf or whatever it is we like to do best. When this happens to you, certain psychological components fall into place.

1. Your abilities or skills match the challenges you face.
2. You have a deep contact with your strong sides, your inner nature.
3. You are deeply concentrated.
4. You feel a deeply effortless involvement as part of a process smoothly moving forward.
5. Your feeling of self and thoughts such as "I am", "I can" or "I can't" disappear.
6. Your sense of time disappears.

---

[26] Rather than having an aversion or resistance towards these qualities.

The Leader's Mental Scorecard. © Finn Havaleschka.

It is in this state that you fully utilize your potential. For a leader, the task is twofold. First you must try to find your way to the mental state described and then you have to help lay a foundation that will allow your coworkers to find their way to the same state as much as possible. This primarily requires two things. Firstly, your coworkers need to work on tasks and face challenges that match their skills and abilities, and secondly, they need to feel that what they are doing is meaningful. This takes leadership and coaching.

One of the best coaches I can think of in this connection is Abraham Maslow. About Maslow, George Leonard wrote: *"To him, man was not a mass of neuroses but a wealth of potential."*[27] Maslow is known for his hierarchy of needs, a pyramid at whose top lies the "self-actualization" of the individual. The state of self-actualization and experiencing total happiness are said to involve harmony, enjoyment, loss of ego and acting with total focus, Maslow based this on his study of personalities such as Albert Einstein, Eleanor Roosevelt, Albert Schweitzer and Thomas Jefferson. What all these and similar personalities have in common is that they are

> *"strongly focused on problems outside of themselves. They generally have a mission in life; they delight in bringing about justice, stopping cruelty and exploitation, fighting lies and untruth. They have a clear perception of reality along with a keen sense of the false, the phony. They are spontaneous and creative, sometime displaying what might be called a mature childlikeness, a "second naiveté". They are autonomous, not bound tightly to the customs and assumptions of their particular culture.........Significantly, they do not lump people or ideas in the usual categories but rather tend to see straight through "the man-made mass of concepts, abstractions, expectations, beliefs and stereotypes that most people confuse with the World".*[28]

Not surprisingly, it appears that many people who are considered to be really excellent leaders possess the same personality traits and moral and con-

---

[27] George Leonard, "Abraham Maslow and the New Self", Esquire, Dec. 1983: 332.
[28] Leonard, 332.

The Leader's Mental Scorecard. © Finn Havaleschka.

science-related values that Maslow uses to describe "the whole self."[29] It is also these people who most often experience moments of self-actualization. Maslow's view is that a whole self is not a person who has had some extra dimensions added to his or her personality; on the contrary, it's someone from whom nothing has been taken. In other words, we all have the potential; it just needs to be allowed to grow. In this, Maslow is completely in line with other developmental psychologists.[30]

But what is it that keeps us from exploiting this potential? Maslow says that, in every situation, we should be aware of what we choose, why we choose it, and especially what we choose *not* to choose. Oddly enough, one of the greatest obstacles to conscious choice is the fact that most of us are so very dependent on other people's perception of us, of who we are, and of what we do. To a great extent, we allow ourselves to be restricted in our reactions and options by the expectations others have of us – and of the expectations we believe they have. In addition, there are the restrictions that lie in our expectations to our own results, to what we want or need to achieve, and thus the reward on one hand and/or the difficulties or negative sanctions we expect on the other. Perhaps we worry too much about this area. Once, Mark Twain is supposed to have said,

> I've had many troubles in my life,
> most of which never happened.

You're worried about making it on time, about whether what you're doing is good enough, whether you are pushing other people away, whether others

---

[29] Finn Havaleschka, The Successful Manager – How Do We Know (Risskov, Denmark: Garuda Research Institute, 2002). Can be downloaded from www.garudahr.com.

[30] As you have probably already guessed, I do not share this perception any longer. I don't believe that self-actualization comes automatically, as the needs we have according to Maslow's heirarchy of needs are fulfilled, or that there are some traits that are suppressed as we are growing up. As far as I can see, some people are more predisposed to the type of behavior and the human qualities that are described as self-actualization or that lead to that state. Ghandi, Einstein, Schweitzer, Roosevelt, and Jefferson, whom Maslow studied – and, for that matter, Maslow himself – already exhibited in childhood the qualities in their personalities that made them world famous. Of course, you could probably find examples of a horribly inappropriate (unloving) childhood having suppressed the development of the qualities of self-actualization, but I am also certain that you could find just as many examples of people exhibiting self-actualizing behavior in spite of a lack of love while they were growing up. However, this belief of mine does not keep me from having the attitude that I will always strive to influence my children and treat my fellow human beings in such a way as to stimulate self-actualizing behavior and all the splendid qualities associated with it. Still, I believe it is important that we begin to differentiate between facts and hope.

like you, whether your kids will do well, whether you've found the right path, whether your wife will leave you, what they are saying about you, whether you will also have a job tomorrow, whether you will have enough money to live on when you retire, whether you will get the job you applied for, whether you will win or lose, whether you have enough gasoline for the trip – and you could keep on adding to the list, and it could go on forever. A lot of what we are worried about every day are things that we really can't do very much about. Once the cards are played and the decisions have been made, we can do no more. We can observe and maybe intervene if time and events show that we're not on the right path. Worry ties up our energy and thus our ability to act constructively and exploit our entire potential. Worries restrict us and keep us from initiating proactive behavior, i.e. behavior that we control ourselves, not behavior dictated by our personality-ruled autopilot.

Avoiding needless anxiety, then, must be the first step towards the ability to change your behavior. About the other things that impede development, Maslow writes:

> "We must become more fully aware of the fixative and regres-
> sive power of ungratified deficiency-needs, of the attractions of
> safety and security, of the functions of defense and protection
> against pain, fear, loss, and threat, of the need for courage in
> order to grow ahead"[31].

Personally, I don't like the phrase "*and protection against pain, fear, loss, and threat...*". There is too much psychology of suffering in that wording. Pain, loss and threats! Perhaps what I have against it is I think the wording implies a general attitude that it is all just an illness. It seems as though a description of inappropriate behavior, unpleasant feelings and negative mental states can or must always be based on a person's painful experiences, e.g. losing something they held dear or serious threats to health, life and soul.

At any rate, it is our doubts about the future and our efforts to hold onto the degree of security, safety, love, understanding, acceptance and conside-ration that we feel we have now that keep us from changing our behavior and learning something new about ourselves.

---

[31] Abraham Maslow, Toward a Psychology of Being, (New York, Van Nostrand, 1968), 46.

To put it more simply,

**W**here we feel safest and most secure,
that's where we want to stay.

However, that is not necessarily the place where development happens. A results-oriented leader, a Red leader, feels safest employing Red leadership. He has difficulty imagining that there could be more security and happiness waiting for him if he tried practicing Green (Development), Blue (Integrator) or Gray (Baser) leadership.

What is it, then, that promotes development? Maslow believes that we do not develop and change because some psychologist or other says it would be a good idea, because someone asked us to, because it would make us live longer, because it would be good for humankind, because we would be rewarded for it, or because it is the logical thing to do. We develop and grow for exactly the same reasons why we choose one dessert over the other, or because kissing one person gives us greater pleasure than kissing another person, or because being friends with Person A is more subjectively satisfying to us than being friends with Person B. All the choices we make in life are what make us learn about ourselves: what we like and don't like, and what we are good at and what we're not good at.

*"This is the way in which we discover the Self and the answer to the ultimate questions Who am I? What am I?"*[32].

The way I see it, we make the choices we do because we *hope* or *believe* that what we choose will make us happier, give us greater satisfaction, and/or ensure that security, happiness and satisfaction won't be taken from us. However, happiness – or feeling happy – is not necessarily the reason for our existence. The hunt for happiness is the force that drives us forward towards new experiences and thus towards developing the ability to exploit our full potential. Then, when we finally seem to have found happiness – with a spouse, friend, job, car, house, or position, or with things as they are – then we feel safe and secure.[33] And that's fine, but the danger is that then we stay right where we are, afraid to lose what we've got, and all development stops.

---

[32] Leonard, 45.

[33] See Finn Havaleschka, In Search of Leadership, (Risskov, Denmark: Garuda Forlag, 1990), 214.

During our lifetime, we fluctuate between two poles. Maslow illustrated it as shown in Scheme 1, except that I added the Head-Heart-Legs figure in the middle:[34]

## Scheme 1. The balance between security and growth

| Security | ← → | | → | Growth |
|---|---|---|---|---|
| Bad things are waiting for me just around the corner. If I lose this (.....), some of my happiness will be taken from me. I risk my existence becoming more uncertain and insecure. Reacting to maintain the status quo. Reactive behavior. Reacting to events. | | | | More happiness is just around the corner. If I receive, buy, achieve, experience this (.........), I will become happier and my life will be safer and more secure. Doing things that change the status quo. Proactive behavior. Initiating events. |
| Development strategy: Seeing the risk of not doing anything. Minimizing the attractiveness of maintaining the status quo. The risk of losing (safety, security, happiness) is greater if you don't do anything than if you choose to do something. And exactly what is it that is so wonderful about your life right now? | | | | Development strategy: Seeing the great things you can achieve or obtain by doing something. Minimizing the perception of danger by doing something. The chances of you making your dreams (education, job, love, etc.) come true are good if you do something. It doesn't cost anything to try! |

[34] I developed this so-called "Head-Heart-Legs" model back at the beginning of the 1980s, when I developed the Profile Analysis, a personality test used in connection with recruitment and personal development. The Head illustrates our way to tackle and deal with problems. The Heart stands for the nature of the relations we establish with others, and the Legs illustrate the will we apply to implementing the solutions we choose. You could also say that we use our head to come up with ideas for solutions, our heart to sell the ideas, and our legs to put them into practice. How we do this is determined by our personality. To put it roughly, our intellectual approach to problems is either logical and left-brained or intuitive and right-brained. The nature of the relations we establish with others is more or less influenced by introvertedness/extrovertedness and trust/mistrust, and the way we implement solutions is more or less influenced by the need to perform, the will to make a difference, and robustness. These personality trait combinations are what determine which of the four focus areas we focus on in everyday life because our personality is how it is. I will come back to this connection later.

The Leader's Mental Scorecard. © Finn Havaleschka.

**Security**, the box on the left side, is equivalent to stagnation or regression. **Growth**, the box on the right side, is equivalent to development, finding yourself, and learning to live in harmony with yourself, in harmony with your inner nature, independent of the expectations of those around you.

According to Maslow, the development strategy you can use to get away from Security is to make yourself aware of the dangers of things that are safe while minimizing the attractiveness of Security. The way to promote growth is to magnify the attractiveness of Growth and minimize the perception of danger. Maslow and Kierkegaard are probably in agreement:

You have to dare to lose your foothold to move forward.

Maslow puts forward three criteria that the self-actualizing person fulfills. At the same time, these criteria indirectly tell us what stands in the way of acting in a self-actualizing way. Self-actualizing people act and make decisions:

1. **Independently of the good opinions of other people.**
   This does not mean that you don't listen, try to get an idea of, or take into consideration the opinions or expectations of other people; just that, in the end, you make the decision you do because you believe it is the best choice.

2. **Without any thought of gaining power over other people.**
   In other words, you do not seek to affect other people's choices because you want to be noticed, because you want status, or because you want other people to do something they basically don't want to.

3. **Emotionally independent of the results of your efforts.**
   The philosophy here is that your results are a consequence of what you say and do and thus the consequence of a process. If the results turned out differently than expected, then it's a waste of energy to become angry, cross, or depressed, or yell at someone, give others the blame, etc. The result itself is not interesting: It is the process that is of interest. If you focus on the results, then you are not paying attention to the process. The results are merely feedback on the process.

And how do you bring yourself in line with these rules of existence? How do you get around the obstacles that impede the way to developing your potential, aside from avoiding unnecessary worrying? A student once asked Maslow that question. After having understood the three basic values listed above, he asked, "How can I be sure I'll make decisions that will bring me into compliance with the three criteria?"

"It's easy," replied Maslow. "Before you comment, act, and decide what to do, then stop and ask yourself: 'If I do this or say that, *will that bring me at peace?*'"

Here are a few main things to be aware of that may help you get more out of your work with Focused Leadership and the Mental Scorecard.

. . . . . . . . . . . . . . . . . . . . . . . . . . . . . . . . . . . . . . . . . . . . . . . . . . . . . . . . . . . . . . . . .

1. You must learn to make your choices independently of other people's opinions and their positive or negative expectations. You are not a leader in order to impress others.
2. You must learn to focus on the process, live in it, and be a part of it.
3. You must learn to see and understand that the results of your choices and what you do are feedback on the process, i.e. on why you got those results. Adjust your next decision and your behavior accordingly.
4. You must learn not to worry.

. . . . . . . . . . . . . . . . . . . . . . . . . . . . . . . . . . . . . . . . . . . . . . . . . . . . . . . . . . . . . . . . .

Look at life as a process of learning, and consider the following philosophy:

> *"No matter what you choose to do, in principle you never do anything wrong. "Mistakes" and "wrong" don't exist. In some situations you simply do not learn quite as easily or quickly as you or others might wish."*[35]

By that, I mean that if you choose to look at life as a learning process, there

---

[35] Finn Havaleschka, On...Development, Life and Leadership (Risskov, Denmark: Garuda Forlag, 1997), 8.

will never be anything you can reproach yourself for, be angry at yourself for, feel guilty about, or worry about. If everything always went in accordance with your ambitions, your expectations or those of others, or your degree of patience, and if you always exhibited the exact same behavior and focused on the same qualities, then you would in reality be standing still. There would be no learning and no development of your potential. The only time when it is reasonable for you to reproach yourself for something or to be worried is if you don't stop and try to figure out why a decision or a certain type of behavior did not give you "peace of mind" and did not bring you along the path you desire to tread.

The result, people's reactions – positive as well as negative – and what makes you angry, irritated, sad, or unhappy are not relevant. It is the process and what you learn from the process that is the core. There are no miraculous ways to forget everything about your own expectations or those of others, or to forget everything about the result, the reactions of others, or getting fired from your job. The most important way is to remain in the process and to be aware of what you choose to focus on. If you are in doubt as to what to choose while you are in the process, then stop and ask yourself, "If I choose to yell at someone, pressure someone, give in, or avoid the problem by only telling part of the truth, will it give me peace of mind?" Likewise, if the results or feedback you got was not what you had planned, hoped for or expected, then stop for a few seconds and ask yourself, "Now what did I learn from that?"

The idea is to be in contact with your intuition, to have the feeling that something feels right. When your inner voice is silent and does not object, then you can assume you are on the right track. If it feels wrong, however, and if your inner voice is expressing doubt, then you can be sure that the choice you are making is not the optimal one. Learning to listen to your inner voice is the best way to help you remain within the process.

In the movie *Ronin*, actor Robert De Niro has the following line:

## When there is a doubt, there is no doubt!

In other words, if you are in doubt, then there is actually no doubt – that you are **not** on the right track. If you are in doubt, you should reconsider what you are about to do or say. Keep a picture of the Focus Model in your mind. Put yourself in the middle of the Model and consider your alternatives. When you imagine yourself standing in the middle and you have an overview of the four courses of action, then ask yourself the question, "If I now went into the Blue area, would it bring me peace of mind?" If you are in doubt, then imagine yourself in your imagination going into the next field, e.g. the Green one, and ask yourself the same question again. Having practiced this technique for a couple of years, I can say that it actually works. I don't always succeed in stopping myself before choosing: my automatic choices are almost always Green or Red. In other words, sometimes feelings come first, or sometimes I am too impatient. But when I do manage to choose one of the other areas, I most often immediately get positive feedback of one kind or another. Sometimes you don't find out that the decision was the correct one until several months afterwards. The seed *was* sewn, but while doubt nags and you say to yourself that maybe you shouldn't have chosen a Green solution after all, you can't see that the seed has taken root and is beginning to sprout. You don't discover it until the fruit has ripened and fallen to the ground.

The next and last general rule that you should learn to use is as follows:

> The only way to free yourself of one thought
> is to replace it with another one.

We are all familiar with situations in which we become worried, begin to think negatively, and act non-constructively, situations in which your thoughts start a downward spiral, and you might have a pessimistic and depressively heavy feeling or take inappropriate action. The only way to break the cycle is to consciously replace that thought with another one. However, just telling yourself to think of something else, to think of something positive is not enough. The thought that you intend to replace the inexpedient thought with must contain more energy than the thought you want to replace. Thus this new thought has to be related to something or make you think of something that you can feel, hear, sense, smell or taste. This new thought must be able to put images and colors on our your inner television screen and start a flow of warm, positive thoughts. Perhaps all you need is a thought that can bring a smile to your lips and thus kick-start production of endorphines, the hormone that makes us feel happy. But, of course, that's not just something you do; it requires practice. We must make ourselves aware of it, and we must practice replacing a dominating thought with another one, doing so both mentally and in practice. Do not just let your spotlight run the show.

Take the following example. How do you react when one of your coworkers comes too late, or is not properly prepared to handle the situation, or when it is clear that he or she hasn't prepared himself or herself properly? My reaction is to become surly, irritated and angry. My feeling automatically causes a fairly strong reaction that I won't explain here. And when I'm in the middle of that reaction, I know that in most cases by far, my reaction is inappropriate. But what should I do when my Development and Results gene kicks in?! This is where the exercises come in, along with the idea that unless you have imagined something in your own inner universe, you will have difficulty putting it into practice. Take pilots, who during their training practice a number of emergency procedures that they can later carry out almost by reflex if the alarm light goes on. We have to do the same thing. Before the situation arises, we have to practice how we will tackle it when it does arise – not *if* it arises, because it definitely will. In other words, we have to know in advance and we have to have practiced the alternative to the inappropriate thought or behavior that does not give us "peace of mind." It's not enough just to say that you'll have to do it better next time. You have to practice before the next time comes. The only problem is that the number and complexity of possible situations and possible alternative actions make everything seem well nigh impossible to gain an overview of. For this reason, we need a model so we can categorize both situations and alternative action and thus create such an overview. And that is exactly the purpose of the Focus Model, which I will now explain in greater detail.

# III. The Focus Model
## The four Focus Areas of Leadership

The purpose of the Focus Model is to give you an image that you can store away in your memory, your inner archive, and store so well that you will be able to pull it out at any time, even in high-pressure and emotionally charged situations, and see what your options are for action. Basically, what you focus on as a leader – your approach to leadership and life in general – depends on your temperament, your personality and your attitude towards what it means to be a leader. For the sake of simplicity, we can divide people's approach to leadership into four categories, or areas:

The first approach is represented by **the Baser area** in the lower left-hand corner of the model. The focus of people who take this approach is on order, systematization, limits, structures, safety/certainty, details, creating predictability by making and following plans, organizing, calculating, and checking.

Moving to the right, the next area is the Results area. In this approach, the focus is on obtaining actual results. This is where you consciously put pressure on yourself, others, push, take chances, exploit the situations of the moment, are impatient, get straight to the point and sometimes go over the line. You consciously choose to work with a short-term view and with the attitude that things have to be done right now.

The third approach is **the Integrator area**, in the upper right-hand corner. When you take this approach, your focus is on interaction between people, avoiding conflicts, creating consensus, understanding others, and getting others to understand. This is where you look at what other people's expectations are and try to find out what motivates them.

I call the fourth area **the Development area**. People focused on this area are busy thinking up and formulating concepts, values and visions. They take the longer view, experiment with new thoughts and ideas, and seek a greater understanding of backgrounds and contexts. See figure 7.

## Figure 7. The four leadership focus areas

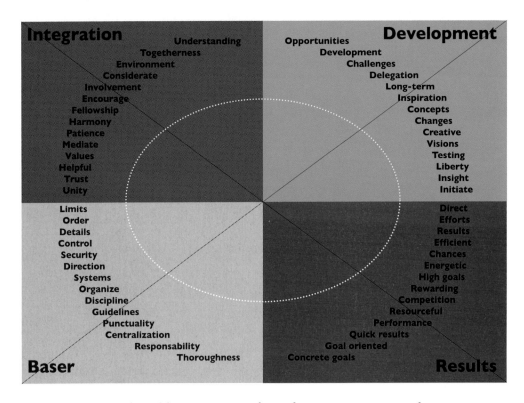

In the real world, we move our focus from one area to another to a greater or lesser extent, depending on our personality. It's not something we spend a lot of time thinking about; it happens automatically. Most of us are primarily focused on one or two areas, but overlook or even have a clear aversion to one or two of the other focus areas. Some people love to work with the big picture, with visions and strategies, but it goes against the grain for them to think in terms of systems, limits, following certain rules, security and details. Others lavish attention on their social environment and their working relationships and have absolutely no focus on pushing, pressuring and taking chances. However, if we only focus on the Development and Integration areas, for example, things often go no further than talking about visions, the future and new ideas. Getting things moving, creating the right conditions and getting results get pushed into the background. On the other hand, if our focus is only on laying the groundwork, writing the rules and getting immediate results, then the social environment, communicating the overall objective, and renewal are pushed into the background. If this happens, then your process is in trouble.

Our model enables us also to look at leadership as a process with four areas. Sometimes we are focused on leading other people so they have and follow certain rules and procedures when they do their work. I call that having a **Baser** focus, because it is about getting basic, everyday things to work or function right. At other times, we focus on how we can reach the goals we set faster, more efficiently and using fewer resources. I call that having a **Results** focus.

Basic things have to be in place before you can create results. Sometimes, in between all these activities, perhaps we stop to think about a conflict we had with a colleague or a disagreement with a subordinate, and try to figure out how we best can rebuild our working relationship into a good collaborative one. This is what I call having an **Integrator** focus. Among other things, Integrator leadership is about ensuring understanding within the organization that it is necessary for some basic structures to exist within which results-creating processes can and must unfold. Integrator leadership connects Baser activities with Results activities. Lastly, if you are thinking about various suggestions as to how you best can market a new product or how you can use new approaches, thoughts and ideas to take your department or organization forward to a more advantageous position, I call that having a **Development** focus.

Thus the four focus areas are connected to each other. **Development leadership** is about formulating new objectives and developing new concepts, methods and rules (i.e. new Baser qualities) and developing the processes and activities needed to achieve the objectives (i.e. new Results qualities). **Baser leadership** is about setting up and arranging things so that results can be created. **Results leadership** is about starting up and controlling the results-creating processes and activities. **Integrator leadership** is about obtaining acceptance and understanding of the new goals, concepts, methods and rules and ensuring that everyone accepts and understands the processes and activities that are necessary.

The more aware we are of changing focus and doing it at the right time with respect to the coworker in question and the situation, the closer we get to good leadership. When we observe people and use a personality profile to ask them which of the four focus areas they work most with, don't think so

The Leader's Mental Scorecard. © Finn Havaleschka.

much about, or don't pay attention to at all, we get some clear pictures. Some people primarily focus on one of the areas, many focus on two of the areas, and a very few focus on three. Almost no one has a focus on all four areas. In addition, most people not only have no focus on one or two of the areas; they *choose* not to focus on them. Personality and temperament determine

1  what you focus on and the way you view and handle what you focus on,
2  the type of the social relations you establish with others, and
3  the will and energy you put into you decide to do.

These statements about focus refer to the Head-Heart-Leg model. The Head-Heart-Leg model is based on the philosophy that you are approaching problems, generating ideas and organizing the problem solving process using your Head. Problem solving is Head-work. But Head-work is not enough; you need to get an acceptance on your idea and your way of solving the problem, and that's Heart-work. And finally, you need to implement your idea, your solution, and that's Leg-work. You can be good at Head-work, but it won't work if you are not so good in Heart or Leg-work. In managerial positions you need to have a balanced Head-Heart-Leg work.

## Figure 8. The Head-Heart-Leg model

Head Work:
Creating ideas for how to solve problems

Heart Work:
Establishing relations, getting ideas accepted

Leg Work:
Implementing ideas, creating results

*This model is copyrighted and a registered trademark by Garuda Research Institute.*

The Leader's Mental Scorecard. © Finn Havaleschka.

Usually the more creative person characterized by personality traits like system flexibility, comprehensiveness, abstract thinking and risk willingness prefer to focus on Development leadership, the more linear thinking person stronger on personality traits like order, detail, security, self control more or less automatically focus on Baser leadership, the person with strong social traits like empathy, social contact, trust et cetera focus on Integrator leadership and finally the person with strong ego traits like competition, influence, self confidence, robustness more or less automatically focus on Result leadership.

As stronger the traits, as more difficult it seems to be for a person to change focus. And, as more balanced a person is, as easier he or she can flex between the 4 kind of leadership focus.

Your placement on a given personality trait within the 3 categories, Head-Heart-Leg, can be registered with a personality test, which in this book is too complex. Hence the Focus model. If you are mostly to the more detail oriented and systematic left brainwork, then you are probably most for Baser leadership. If your are mostly achievement oriented and competitive, impatient, taking chances – creating chances, then you are more for Result leadership. If you are more in your heart, sensing and feeling the mood and expectations created in human relations, then you are probably mainly for Integrator leadership.

And finally, are you more the right brain type of person, creative, experimenting, acting impulsive and with imagination, then you are probably more for Development leadership.

But it doesn't matter what type you are, the most important is to know and accept where you are, there is a need for all of us. In the same way as the model describes the four leadership styles, it also describes four leadership functions, i.e. four functions or areas that typically involve tasks that can be described using the model and best handled using one of the leadership styles described. What follows is an example of how these areas are connected, as told by the CEO of a small manufacturing business with 40 employees.

> *I was on my way to work one day, and I was thinking – as*
> *always – about what I had to have done by the end of the day.*
> *I was supposed to check some key financial and production*

*figures, and I also had to check whether the rules that we had agreed on some time ago for recording incoming orders had been implemented and were working. The most important thing I had to do – but also the most boring thing – was to go through our existing partnership contracts and make sure that some of the terms were changed in future contracts. What was boring about the work was that I myself had to write the rules that were going to apply.*

With this focus, the company CEO was practicing **Baser leadership**. The CEO was focusing on some areas that contained the same qualitative elements. These tasks were specific, the type that is best handled if you set up and follow certain rules and if you are systematic, structured, security-oriented, precise, etc. At the same time, this is the kind of absolutely basic thing that *has* to be done if the company is to function. That's why I call them **Baser** tasks, and Baser tasks require Baser leadership.

The CEO to continue his description:

*Once I got to the office, though, it quickly became clear that I wasn't going to have much time to concentrate on what I had planned to do. A customer had just given us the green light to go ahead with an order we had worked hard to land – if we could fill the order within 30 days. That was a problem that I had to handle. So the production manager and I sat down and concentrated on changing priorities and production plans, and contacted other customers to ask them if it was all right if we delayed their shipments a little. At the same time, it was also necessary for me to ask some workers to speed up their work process. We needed to rev things up, and we had to find some solutions so that this peak load and our payroll costs wouldn't ruin the financial side of the project.*

With this focus, the CEO was practicing **Results leadership**. He was concentrating on the tasks that involve the same qualitative elements as described above, tasks that best be described in terms such as results, short-term, tangible goals, goal-oriented, fast-paced, move and push – tasks that are best solved with a slightly impatient attitude and a willingness to take risks to some degree. At the same time, it is work that *has* to be done if the company is to continue to exist. They are **Results** tasks. To be able to perform these tasks, certain basic structures have to be in place, and Results tasks require Results leadership.

> *In the 30 days it took to complete the order, every so often I just had to stop. Several of our workers felt that the pressure and responsibility got to be too much, so I had to spend quite a bit of time focusing on getting everyone to work together, talking with them about what had to be done, give them time and room to discuss the situation and the different problems they had. I had to force myself to be more patient, make encouraging remarks, listen, give advice, etc.*

When he had this focus, our CEO was practicing **Integrator leadership**: yet another leadership function and one that was qualitatively different from the first two mentioned above. He was focusing on **Integrator** tasks, whose purpose was to create team spirit and understanding and allow people to work together and exchange information, opinions and advice. His job here was to make the basic structure and the process of obtaining results function, and this often requires a leader to be patient and understanding and to show empathy and listen, among other things.

Performing this kind of task requires Integrator leadership; without it, any organization will quickly tumble into a crisis, as you can probably well imagine. Baser tasks and Results tasks are qualitatively very different and are therefore often carried out by very different types of people: e.g. security-oriented technicians and risk-taking sales representatives respectively. People that are good at Baser work are normally structure- and detail-oriented, but salespeople are generally process- and results-oriented, and Integrator leadership is a must if you want these two sets of qualities to mesh and work together.

> *And while I was alternating between focusing on the needs of my subordinates, working with the partnership contract and trying to get the order finished on time, I couldn't, of course,*

*help thinking about strategies for selling our new product. The future of the company depended on this product, so I walked around with my notebook and jotted down an outline of my thoughts and ideas. When I had time, I talked with various people inside and outside the company about my ideas. At the end of the day, marketing, development and strategy are my job, you know.*

With this focus, our CEO was practicing **Development leadership**, and the tasks connected with this type of leadership can be described using the same concepts: development, strategy, concepts, future, long-term change, innovation, etc. These tasks we call **Development** tasks, and they are best handled using Development leadership, which means the leader allows himself and others a great deal of mental, intellectual and emotional freedom to give their creativity free rein, be innovative and keep an open mind.

As we have seen, this CEO moves his focus from function to function. And, just like in real life, only to a certain degree is it he himself that decides what type of leadership he employs and what function he is focusing on at any one time.

This is not because he does not know what he is doing. He had certain plans, but then reality got in the way and he had to improvise. He reacted on the basis of his experience, empathy, intuition, impressions and temperament: the traits that are characteristic for his personality. At the same time, he apparently moved easily from Results leadership to Integrator leadership, from Baser leadership to Development leadership, and so on back and forth from function to function, changing his style to match the function in question, the objective and what he wanted to achieve.

At the same time, it shines through his description that Baser leadership – and Integrator leadership to some degree as well – is not what he likes to do best, but he acknowledges the necessity of being able to practice it.

*That* is what a good leader can do and actually does. The good leader is in balance, using his or hers Head, Heart or Leg qualities in accordance to the need of the situation.

How would you prioritize if you were in the same situation? My point is that different people react differently to the same situation. Presumably, we have the same goal – to get that big order and make sure it gets delivered on time – but our ways of reaching that goal will be different. Even if we could predict all possible consequences of every single choice and every single prioritization, each of us would still choose or prioritize differently. A Results leader would focus on expanding capacity and speeding up the process. An Integrator leader would be very aware of the human and social consequences of pushing up the pace and the extra responsibility he gives his subordinates. A Baser leader would focus on structuring things and making plans and calculations so that he feels he has everything under control. And, fourth but not least, a Development leader would do everything he could to find time to work with ideas for marketing the new product and describing the new concept, and maybe also come up with a plethora of ideas about how to deliver the order on time – without otherwise taking any kind of direct responsibility upon himself.

For most of us, it is true that our leadership style is so deeply anchored in our personality that we don't normally see it or think about alternatives in any kind of detail. It's not that we are unconscious of our options; we just don't think about them consciously and deal with them. We practice what I call leadership "in an absence of awareness."

Thus the first step on the road to Focused Leadership is getting to know yourself: being aware of your normal style, the one determined by your personality and temperament, and thus also aware of your immediate reaction patterns. With that, you also become aware of the alternatives you exclude or deselect because they're just not you, because you have a certain aversion towards them, or simply because it simply doesn't occur to you that those alternatives exist.

The next step is learning to be aware of the effect you have on other people. There is nothing new in the fact that different people perceive you differently. Sometimes you wonder how A can stand working together with B, for example. But it's not a problem for B, because she sees A from a different point of view than you or I do.

Thus we are constantly subjected to other people's interpretations and evaluations, but often unaware of it. Even if we are aware of it, we do not realize in some situations that we are seen and judged differently than we see ourselves or than we think others see us.

This fact is another element of the concept of "absence of awareness." Perhaps you don't think about it, but most people do react to your management style, your appearance, your charm and your physical presence more than they react to where you want to lead them, your intentions or your message. In other words, we react more to a person and the way they are than we react to what he or she wants. As we know, but often forget:

Before other people tune into what you are saying - your ideas, they tune into what you exude.

You could say that we often react faster and more strongly to form than we do to content. For this reason, being aware of how you are regarded and perceived – your effect on other people – is just as important a prerequisite to practicing Focused Leadership as being aware of the leadership style you have and the leadership tasks you are using that leadership style on. If you are not aware of how other people see you, it is easy to fail to communicate properly with others.

When you are unable to have a constructive dialog with them about what you want, it is hardly likely that they will do what you want them to do.

There is only one way to find out how other people perceive you: by asking, observing, discussing and reasoning. Perhaps people *do* see you as you are: a systematic, disciplined and responsible person with everything under control in most situations.

All of these are positive characteristics, especially seen with your own eyes, naturally. However, if you look at the behavior and attitude behind it all with *other* eyes, e.g. green Developer eyes (see the model), then it is easier to see the negative sides of these characteristics: an inflexible, controlling leader who runs everything according to schedules and rules, with no room for experimentation or creativity. With this, I am simply pointing out something we all know:

What you see is in the eye of the beholder.

A Gray leader doesn't see the same when he is practicing Blue leadership as a Blue leader does – or, for that matter, as a Green or Red leader does. Your evaluation and view of another leader also depend on the area in which you yourself are standing. For example, seen from the Blue area, a Red leader looks like an impatient, brash and maybe even slightly ruthless type of manager; seen from the Gray area, he looks like someone who oversteps their bounds and ignores rules, limits and agreements if they don't suit him. If you are standing in the Green area, you see this Red leader as a goal-oriented, stubborn person that finds it difficult to change tracks and find new pathways, and is thus also unable to take a strategic approach.

We can use the model to make us aware of these mechanisms, and Figure 9 is an illustration of how they work.

## Figure 9. How a Red leader is perceived

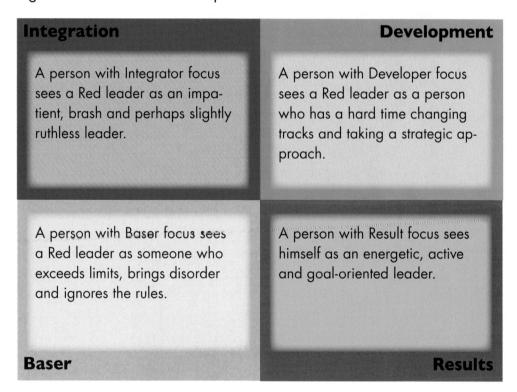

**Integration**

A person with Integrator focus sees a Red leader as an impatient, brash and perhaps slightly ruthless leader.

**Development**

A person with Developer focus sees a Red leader as a person who has a hard time changing tracks and taking a strategic approach.

A person with Baser focus sees a Red leader as someone who exceeds limits, brings disorder and ignores the rules.

A person with Result focus sees himself as an energetic, active and goal-oriented leader.

**Baser**

**Results**

Now, picture the model. Each type of leadership has its own color: Gray for Baser leadership, Red for Results leadership, Blue for Integrator leadership, and Green for Development leadership.

Look at the key words and phrases in the model in Figure 7 to see what kind of leadership is most closely aligned with your personality. The important thing for you to learn now is how to observe the situation you are in, ask yourself what kind of leadership it calls for, and then move yourself away from your normal management style, e.g. Red leadership with a focus on Results leadership, and over to the type of leadership that is ideal for the situation: Gray leadership, for example. In this same way, you can use the model to help find out where your coworkers are: which areas in the model do their personalities put them in? Are they careful workers who feel most comfortable with security, order and structure, or are they a little more devil-may-care and don't mind taking a chance or two here and there.

Whether or not you sympathize with it, you have to go to where your coworkers are and meet them there. You can use the model to find out what kind of leadership the task at hand requires and to shed light on - and possibly liberate yourself from - your more instinctive reactions or aversions and your subjective assessments of the other personality types and types of leadership. And you can use the model as a tool for analysis and diagnosis.

Imagine the following situation. We have a Green leader, i.e. an abstract, creative type of person who is full of new ideas, who learns by experimenting, who has a good overview of things, and who is good at formulating concepts, visions and strategies. On the other hand, he has a difficult time of it if you restrict him too much in how he does his job. He performs best when given a great deal of freedom of thought and action. Let's say this manager is in charge of a worker with a Baser-type personality; in other words, the worker needs order and structure, a workplace and a world in which he can maintain an overview and predict the consequences of his actions and decisions. There has to be some rules and limits set for this person that makes his everyday working life safe and secure. Let's add to the situation the circumstance that this worker is also responsible for developing parts for a new product.

The third element in this Green manager's situation is the "situation" itself, or the task at hand. Due to unforeseen circumstances beyond his control, the worker is behind in developing these new product parts. As a result, he feels insecure and stressed, and everyone is waiting for the Green leader to solve the problem. We can use the model to sketch the situation.

See Figure 10.

# Figure 10. The Leadership Model

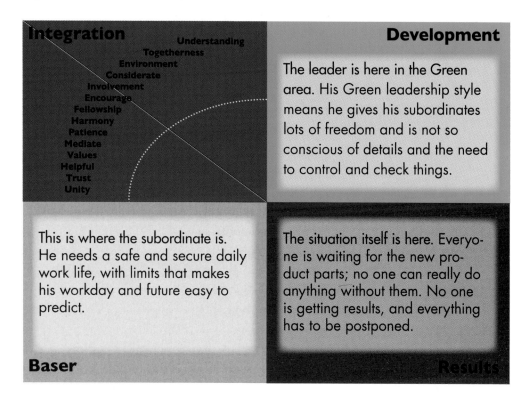

**Integration**

Understanding
Togetherness
Environment
Considerate
Involvement
Encourage
Fellowship
Harmony
Patience
Mediate
Values
Helpful
Trust
Unity

**Development**

The leader is here in the Green area. His Green leadership style means he gives his subordinates lots of freedom and is not so conscious of details and the need to control and check things.

This is where the subordinate is. He needs a safe and secure daily work life, with limits that makes his workday and future easy to predict.

The situation itself is here. Everyone is waiting for the new product parts; no one can really do anything without them. No one is getting results, and everything has to be postponed.

**Baser**

**Results**

Imagine that the subordinate is the only one in the company that has the skills needed to develop those product parts, and the company does not wish to contract this job out for strategic reasons. What would you suggest?

Ideally, the solution is simple. As the Green leader, you must move down into the Gray area and make yourself mentally aware of the needs that govern your subordinate and how he perceives you and your responsibility for the situation he is in. Since you are a Green leader, you can easily imagine that this worker believes that you are largely responsible for him feeling uncertain and insecure about his day-to-day work. Perhaps you do not understand this person because you are the type who experiments his way forward and doesn't lose sleep over a few missing details. But it's not about you right now: it's about your subordinate. You need to find a handle on the situation, a safety harness that will allow this person to relax and believe that what you are doing will ensure him a safe and secure workday environment.

Before you move down into the Gray area, you will have to consider the following. How can you (figuratively) go to the place where your subordinate is? What kind of arguments can reassure him, and what can you do to give him more peace of mind and perhaps the peace and quiet he needs to work efficiently at his job? Once you have acknowledged your own starting point and familiarized yourself with how your subordinate sees the situation, and you have some ideas about how to provide the framework and guarantees necessary to make this person feel safe and secure about doing his job, then you're ready for the next phase.

The next phase is you moving up into the Blue area. This is where you communicate, show consideration and patience (presumably not the thing you are best at, being a Green leader), and you need to listen. The idea is to create trust and understanding. You must be extremely aware of what kind of effect you are having on this person. How does he normally perceive you? You must listen, ask for more details, explain things and show understanding. Once you have reached a mutual understanding, then together you have to figure out what the best possible way is to move you both forward. And then you are both ready for the next phase: moving down into the Red area, where you need to set specific and realistic goals and plans of action.

Try to imagine the process in your own mental awareness (see Figure 11). What is this subordinate like? How does he react to various arguments, and how do you react? How does this person view you? Run the process in your head, mentally. First look at yourself, standing in the Green corner. How do you react? How do you normally solve problems? What kind of needs are you governed by?

Then move down into the Gray corner, your subordinate's corner. How does this person see you, this person with the needs and the way of tackling and handling problems that the key words in the Gray corner describe? What can you do to accommodate this person and his needs?

Now move up into the Blue corner. Ask questions, listen, explain, make suggestions. How can you communicate with this person so that the two of you reach a mutual understanding? Now it's time to move down into the Red corner.

# Figure 11. The leadership process

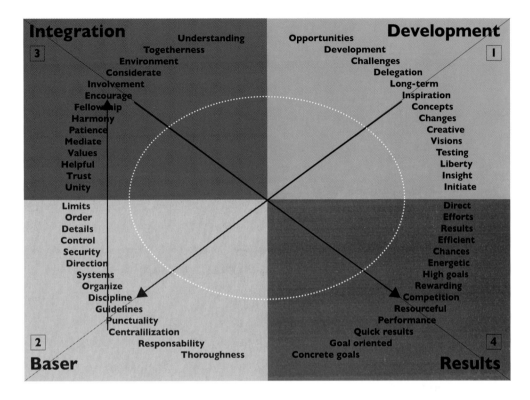

Remember, the more you imagine yourself practicing a certain type of behavior - in your thoughts, in your imagination, on your inner television screen, using your hearing and all your other senses - the greater the chances that you will be able to actually practice this behavior in reality.

In the following I will go into greater detail about how you can transfer the model and principles to your own world and your own leadership style. It's all about mental preparation: mental training in how to think and act differently than you normally do, and to act in accordance with the situation. You don't need to change your personality; you only need to learn to utilize more of the potential you already possess.

# IV. Focused Leadership
## The Personality of the Leader

The Focused Leadership Model is a tool that can help you learn to lead yourself and thus make decisions independently of the opinions and expectations of others, be present in the moment, and see things in a broader context. The four focus areas and matching four leadership styles possess four sets of qualities that you should become familiar with so that you are always aware of the type of leadership you are practicing and so that it is not chance, not your results, not other peoples' expectations, not your mood, and not your sense of self that determines the choices you make.

The idea is for you to learn to feel, be aware of, sense and see the difference between Baser leadership, Results leadership, Integrator leadership and Development leadership. It should feel like it does when you leave your living room and go out your front door into April spring weather. You should be able to feel, smell, sense and see the difference.

To make you more conscious of what you want to focus on and what you may already be doing now, the following provides a more detailed explanation of the four focus areas and personality-determined leadership styles. The following profiles and descriptions have been taken from real life. We will take a look at four managers active today and describe their daily approach to leadership. While you are reading about their different approaches to leadership, remember that the more freedom you give yourself, the easier it will be for you to alternate between the four leadership styles. Also, be aware that none of the four leadership styles and thus none of the managers we describe here are better or more valuable than any of the others. Value comes into the picture when things are put together right.

Leaders who learn to consciously shift from one focus area to another and learn to combine **leadership situation, leadership focus and leadership style** in the right way will have at their command some essential qualifications for leading others. They will possess a mental flexibility which, on balance, will result in more constructive and pleasant hours working together with subordinates and colleagues. This is where we can use Kierkegaard's words about daring to lose one's footing in order to get anywhere. With a little revamping, you could say:

Sometimes we have to let go so that we can hold on.

In other words, you must learn to let go of your usual leadership behavior and, for example, move from Red to Blue leadership to achieve what you want. As one course attendee once said so well: "If you want to develop your relationship with Bonnie, you'll have less time to keep up your relationship with Bess."

The profiles of the four managers below don't just tell us where their focus lies, but also what they more or less consciously choose *not* to focus on. The main focus of the first leader is on Baser leadership, with Results leadership as his secondary focus. Symbolized by the gray color, Baser leadership is generally about focusing on structure, rules, security, instructions and control. If you have a Baser focus, you see that you are good at and don't mind spending time on tasks that require structuring, systematization, planning, and following schedules or plans in which you need to know and stick to certain rules or guidelines or in which you have to measure, weigh and check things. These things could, for example, be physical objects, resources, figures, words or other data that have to be processed, stored, moved and always be at the right place at the right times and in the correct amounts.

Thus Baser leadership requires a focus on security and accuracy right down to the smallest detail. Other key words are precision, order, control, systems, checking, organization, planning, knowing and following rules, instructions, and remaining within given limits and structures.

A more precise description of a profile – or, rather, the person behind the profile – can be made based on that person ranking 56 different statements. Figure 12 is an illustration of such a profile.

## Figure 12. Profile of a Baser leader with a Results focus

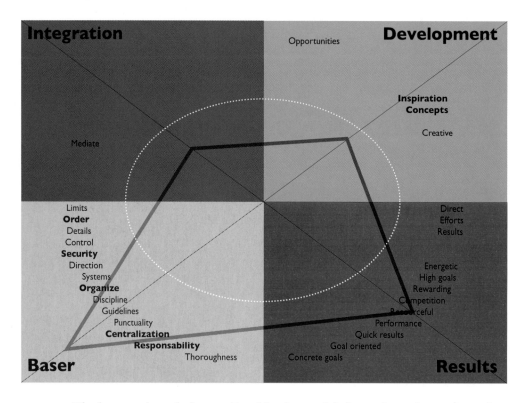

The key words and phrases listed in the model above show the qualities that this manager focuses on. For example, the word "Order" is there – at the top of the gray field – because this person answered that he thought it was very important to *"have systems that create structure, order and discipline"* in the activities of his subordinates. Note that the outline of the profile extends far down into the Gray area, and that there are 14 key words in this area. This tells us that the person answered that he attaches importance to all these elements in his leadership style. For instance, if the key word **"Responsibility"** is in bold print, then this means that the person answered that he thinks it is very important *"to formulate clear guidelines for responsibility and assignments."* In addition to a clear focus on Baser leadership, the profile above also shows that this person also focuses quite a bit on Results leadership. In other words, it is a combination of direction of others, order, and control with being direct, energetic, and results-oriented.

Thus the main ingredients in his leadership style are discipline and results, which can easily turn into a leadership style based on people doing what they're told – at least seen from a Blue subordinate's point of view. What this leader does not focus on can be seen in Figure 13.

## Figure 13. The focus areas the Baser leader rejects

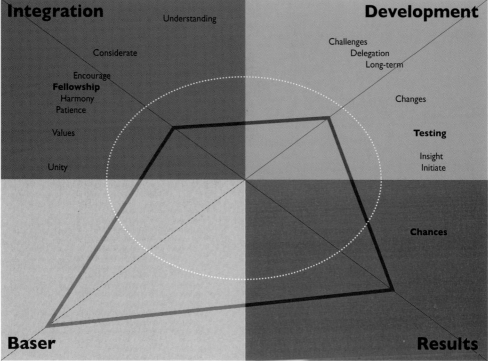

The key words in Figure 13 come from statements in the questionnaire that the manager answered that it was "less important" to do, e.g. he thought it was less important "*to take the time for discussion as needed to get people's support in making a joint effort.*" Judging by this, it is clear that this person's weak sides are a lack of focus on Blue and Green leadership. For this reason, his mental training should consist of learning to apply one or a combination of these two types of leadership, depending on the situation, and doing so not for days or weeks, but just a few minutes or perhaps an hour at a time.

*Baser Leadership is about having everything under control.*

Another typical combination of focus areas is a Results leader who has a secondary focus on Green leadership. Red leadership is about focusing on results. The person behind the next profile, Figure 14, focuses more or less instinctively on work that requires taking action right here and now, work with something happening all the time, and work where he can see the results of his efforts immediately. Thus he typically focuses on tasks where it is important that things are delivered on time, products must be ready on time, and ideas, products and concepts have to be sold or finished right now. For this person, the challenge and motivation lies in the pleasure of optimizing existing resources, obtaining the biggest possible output, and competing with and doing things better than others and reaping the recognition that follows.

Results leadership requires taking specific steps to achieve clearly defined goals within a specified short period of time and by utilizing certain given resources. The key words for this person as a leader are, among others, competition, performance, independence, robust, impatient, efficient and direct. See the key words in the model in Figure 14.

The Leader's Mental Scorecard. © Finn Havaleschka.

## Figure 14. A Results leader with a Development focus

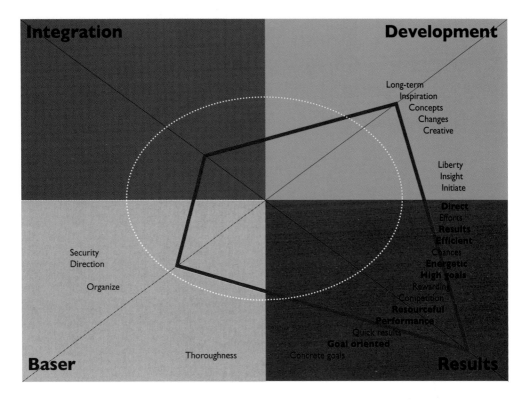

This person's leadership style is governed by concepts such as high goals, energy, goal-oriented, chances, performance, and rewarding. At the same time, the profile shows that there were no positive answers to any statements about Integrator leadership at all. On the other hand, there is a slight emphasis on Baser leadership in the form of control, security and organization, and a little more emphasis on Development leadership, where the focus is on change, initiating things, degrees of freedom, and creativity, among other things. Figure 15 shows what this person attaches less importance to as a leader.

## Figure 15. The focus areas the Results leader rejects

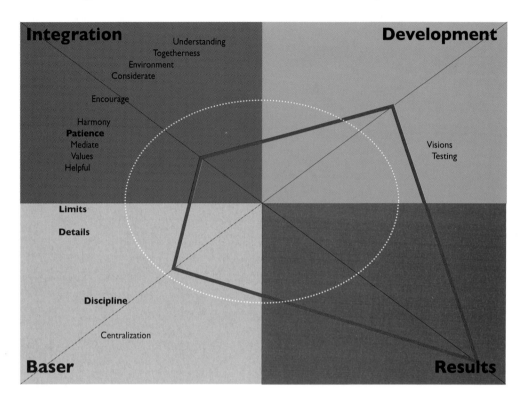

It can be clearly seen from Figure 15 that this person does not attach much importance to the social aspects of leadership. Encouragement, understanding, mediation, helping and being considerate towards others are not a part of his mental consciousness. From the key words in the Gray area, we can see that he doesn't focus a lot on details, setting specific limits or *"leads the way in displaying accuracy, precision and disciplined work"* - he considered it "less important," at any rate. All other things being equal, you might be tempted to conclude that this person focuses only on getting results and not so much on how it's done. In certain situations, this is probably fine, but his focus and the behavior that is a result of this focus are more of a hindrance than a help in ensuring performance of the activities that create results. With this lack of a focus on following certain ground rules – and especially

*Result Leadership is about winning.*

a lack of focus on gaining his coworkers' acceptance and understanding of goals, means and methods – he makes things more difficult for himself (and his coworkers) than they have to be. So in his case, mental training would consist of teaching him to employ Gray and/or Blue leadership, depending on the situation.

The third of the four leader profiles is the Blue leader profile in Figure 16. Blue leadership is primarily employed by Integrator leaders. If you have an Integrator focus, then you like and believe you're good at doing things that ensure that people work well together in their daily work. The manager behind this profile tries to create unity; he works deliberately to avoid discord and conflicts, and he tries to get his coworkers to help each other and stand together. Because he has the personality he does, it is natural for

The Leader's Mental Scorecard. © Finn Havaleschka.

him to be aware of other people's moods, motivation, feelings and needs. He is someone who, with caring and attentive behavior, ensures that people work together – or at least he tries to do so. Thus Integrator leadership requires understanding and patience, and also the ability to hold back on expressing your own points of view, but rather to listen and be sympathetic. A Red leader would probably see this person as too compliant and avoiding conflict; a Gray leader would see a person incapable of and without a sense of order and discipline.

## Figure 16. An Integrator leader with a Development focus

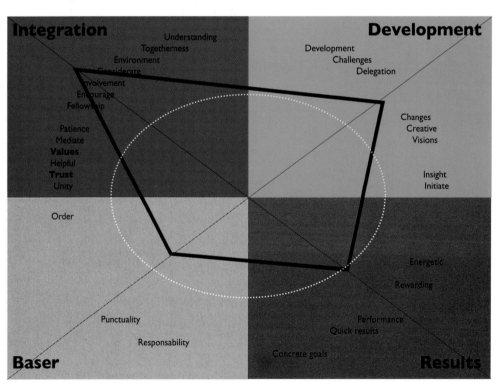

From the key words in the blue area in Figure 16, we can see that this person attaches importance to unity, togetherness, values, encouragement, fellowship, understanding and patience, among other things. At the same time, the profile reveals a certain emphasis on Development leadership: change, challenges, delegation, creative solutions, etc.

From Figure 17 it appears that this person has less focus on Baser and Results leadership. It is mostly Gray leadership that he rejects or avoids: attention to detail, discipline, controlling and centralizing are not things he focuses a great deal on. At the same time, you can see from the Results corner that this is not the type of person that takes chances or sets high goals for himself or his coworkers. At any rate, his answer was that he believed it was less important to "be perceived as the type of leader that sets high goals and never gives up."

This profile (figure 17) and the choices behind it indicate that this person needs to train himself, mentally and in practice, to see more nuances in the various situations that he naturally finds himself in as a result of his leadership duties. He must learn to put himself in the middle of the focus model and objectively assess his options for action.

*Integrator Leadership is about values and togetherness.*

The Leader's Mental Scorecard. © Finn Havaleschka.

Figure 17. The focus areas the Integrator leader rejects

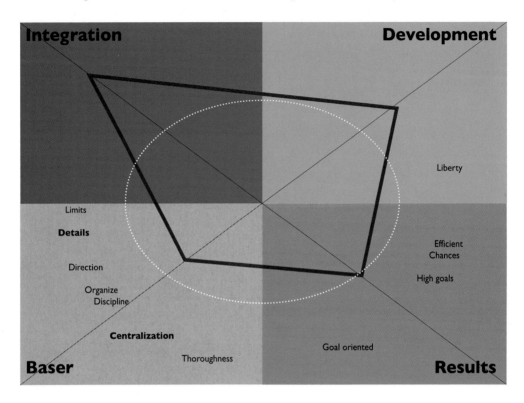

Blue leadership with no requirements as to responsibility, systems and performance level is not always the most suitable choice. He has no focus on the integration of structures and processes: apparently, for him, integration is primarily for the sake of social fellowship.

The last profile I will show you is the profile of a typical Green leader. Green leadership is primarily practiced by a Development leader. If you have a Development focus, you feel you are good at and enjoy spending time on tasks that have to do with strategy, vision, the overall view, and things that take the organization forward. Development tasks are those which produce a qualitative change in existing structures and processes, and thus create a new reality for the company. Examples of such tasks are thinking up and implementing new administrative routines, new ways to manufacture something, new products, new concepts or new ways to sell. And, as can be seen from Figure 18, this is the focus of the last of our four managers.

Good Development leadership requires an overview, creativity, the ability to be visionary, and the ability to communicate and be enthusiastic. The key words are risk, high goals, change, innovation, seeing opportunities, initiating things, seeing the whole picture, formulating concepts, thinking up strategies, creativity, etc.

## Figure 18. A Development leader with a Results focus

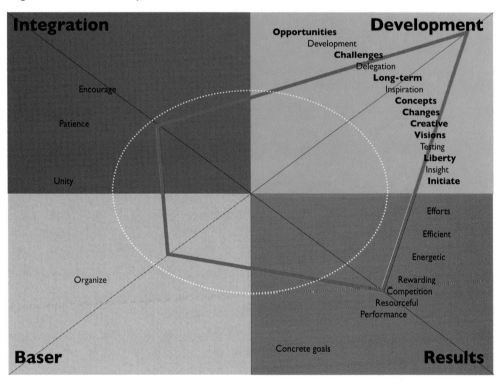

The profile shown in Figure 18 is a good example of a Development leader. From the key words in the Development field, we can see that he attaches importance to being ahead of the pack when it comes to creating change; he focuses on challenges, opportunities, finding creative solutions, vision, etc. At the same time, this person has a certain degree of focus on Red leadership: things must be carried out, demands made and good performance rewarded. On the other hand, there isn't much focus on Integrator leadership and especially little on Baser leadership, as we can see from Figure 18.

## Figure 19. The focus areas the Development leader rejects

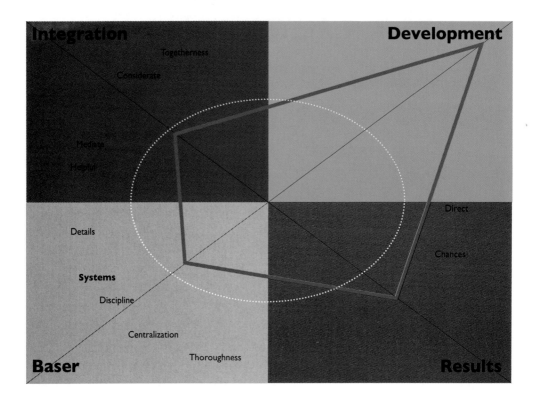

The fact that there are not that many key words in the Gray and Blue fields in Figure 19 is primarily due to this person having indicated "Neutral" as his reaction to the statements that represent those two areas.

Neutral answers are usually a sign that the person is probably aware that these areas are important, but also that they are not something he is terribly interested in. Details and setting up systems so his subordinates always know their duties and the framework within which they are to work, etc. are things this manager - "naturally" - leaves to his subordinates. He certainly is good at delegating, but it's not necessarily something that he does deliberately because he has thought about it and believes that his subordinates have the ability, will or skills necessary to do the work. This delegation may turn

*Development Leadership is about creating opportunities.*

out to be simply a result of his personality, i.e. the absence of any awareness of the necessity and qualities of Blue and Gray leadership.

Mental training and actual practice of Gray and Blue leadership would clearly make everyday life easier for both this leader and his subordinates. When there is a focus on Green and Red leadership, in that order, we often find leaders who run far ahead of their subordinates and the organization, a leadership style that prevailed in the group CEO discussed above.

After this walk-through of the four leaders and their profiles, naturally, you might ask about the truth value of these profiles and thus the descriptions of their strong and weak sides. Of course, the truth value of a profile, i.e. the assessments and thus the starting point for mental training, is no better than the truth of the answers the person gives in the questionnaire, in other words how well he knows himself and whether he is being completely straightforward in his answers. In certain situations, we can have a perception of ourselves, our behavior, our motives and our priorities that may not be shared completely by others. That is why, in most situations, it would be an advantage to allow other people to assess your behavior, motives and priorities. I have written a questionnaire for this purpose that can be filled in by other people so we can make a so-called "360-degree" analysis. In practice,

The Leader's Mental Scorecard. © Finn Havaleschka.

we could ask a manager's own boss to fill in a questionnaire to contribute his assessment, or we could ask the manager's colleagues to give their evaluation, just as we could ask the manager's subordinates to do the same. The idea is simply to create a picture that is as objectively correct as possible to make the person aware of his own focus areas and of the way others see him, thus laying the groundwork for the necessary training.

## The Mirror Profile: Other People's Perceptions

Allow me to introduce you to an example from my own world. The profile below was generated from the questionnaire filled out by Gunnar Nielsen, president and CEO of Garuda Denmark. His job is mainly to head up sales and marketing in Denmark of the HR tools and tests developed by the Garuda Research Institute, of which I am director. In Figure 20 you can see Gunnar's perception of what he focuses on as a leader.

## Figure 20. Gunnar's leadership focus

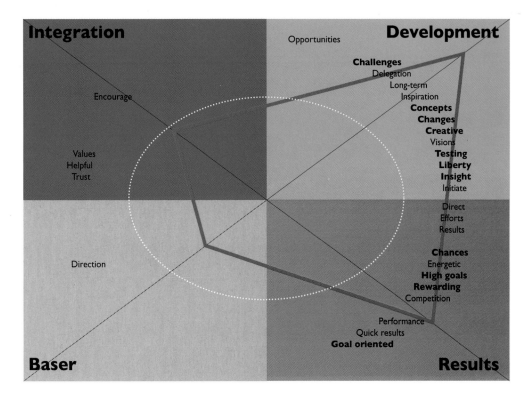

At first glance, it looks good, considering his primary task is marketing. Apparently, he is the type of person that allows himself and others a fair amount of freedom to do their work and get results. This focus is clearly his strong side. But what is it he doesn't focus on?

From the green profile in Figure 21, you can see that Gunnar's opinion and understanding of himself is that he doesn't put a lot of energy into qualities such as togetherness, social harmony, patience with others, order, control and setting up systems. There is almost no focus at all on Gray and Blue leadership.

## Figure 21. The focus areas Gunnar Nielsen rejects

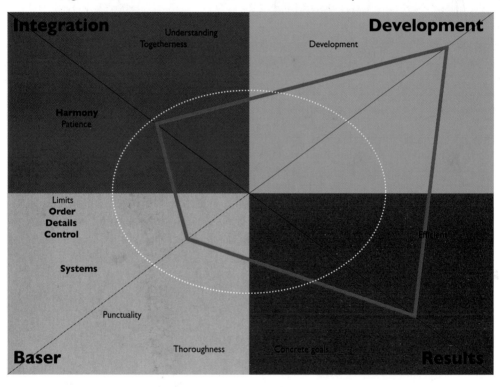

But what do his subordinates say? Do they have the same perception, and if they do, how do they feel about it? Gunnar is in charge of ten workers that handle daily operations and market development, and two of them have contributed feedback on his leadership focus.

The Leader's Mental Scorecard. © Finn Havaleschka.

## Figure 22. How two of his subordinates see Gunnar Nielsen

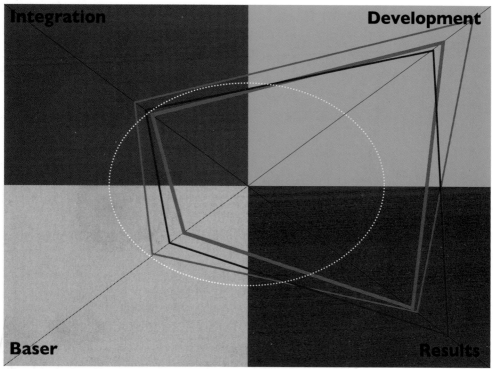

*Gunnar Nielsen's profile is the green bold profile.*

The profile drawn with the thick green line is Gunnar's own. As you can see, there's not a lot of difference between how Gunnar sees himself and his focus and what his subordinates say they see. So far so good. May I say, in all modesty, that Gunnar normally reports to me. Formally and in reality, I'm his boss, and after almost ten years of working together, I think I know him pretty well, which is why the way his subordinates see him came as a bit of a surprise to me. So I also performed my own assessment of his leadership focus. As you can see from Figure 23, the red profile, my perception of Gunnar's focus looks a little different.

My perception is indicated by the profile outlined in a thick red line. My perception is, then, that Gunnar has more focus on Baser leadership than he himself or his two subordinates see. At the same time, I see him as having slightly less focus on the social and integrating aspects of his job. Why? It's because I see Gunnar with my own eyes, from the place where I stand. I am

Figure 23. The way Gunnar's boss views Gunnar's leadership focus

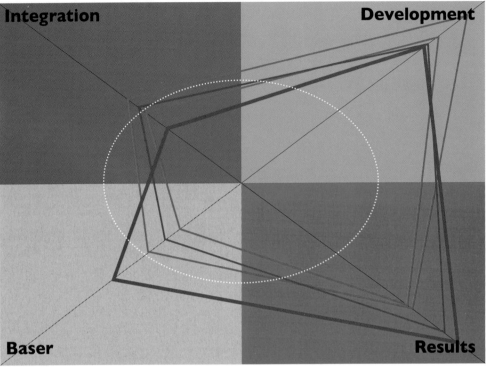

*The way I perceive Gunnar is illustrated by the red profile.*

even more Green in my leadership focus than Gunnar, and that could be one reason. Another reason could be that Gunnar's monthly (highly detailed) reports to our board of directors, of which I am a member, indicate that he has a tremendously structured and systematic work and leadership style. His reports convey the impression that he has everything under control that we expect a man in his position to have under control. However, his subordinates view things a bit differently.

The next question, then, is whether Gunnar, depending on the situation and when there is a need for it, moves his focus to Gray leadership – as I think he does – or to Blue leadership – as I don't see him doing. After talking with Gunnar, however, there is no doubt that actually he does neither, unless he is really under pressure from certain circumstances, e.g. in connection with reporting to the board. He himself feels that he neglects the social aspect of his leadership responsibility. He is not real good at getting the attention of people whose "chemistry" doesn't mix with his, and social chit-chat in general is not really him. He gives people some objectives and a lot of freedom in how they get there, and then lets them do their thing.

Gunnar's subordinates agree with this picture of Gunnar, but they want more time and room for togetherness, time when you discuss shared goals and compare experience. At the same time, it turns out that they also want more guidelines, more structure, and a clearer idea of what is and isn't permitted. Completely to the contrary of what I thought, they feel at a bit of a loss sometimes. We get a clearer idea of what the matter is when we look at the actual questions and answers.

Above are two of the 14 questions asked in the different questionnaires. The first and third questions are the wording used in the leader's questionnaire, who has the option of answering that he focus "A lot," "To some degree,"

| As a leader I put emphasis on: (Double click to edit) | A lot | To same degree | Neutral | Not much | Not at all |
|---|---|---|---|---|---|
| To ensure myself that everyone knows and lives up to the demand for punctuality and precision | | | | ✓ | |
| To ensure him/herself that I know and live up to the demands for punctuality and precision | | | | | Anonymous<br>Anonymous |
| To ensure myself that everyone remains inside the agreed upon limits or use of time and resource. | | | | ✓ | |
| To ensure him/herself that everyone remains inside the agreed upon limits or use of time and resource. | | | | Anonymous<br>Anonymous | |

"Neutral," "Not much" or "Not at all." The leader's answers are indicated by check marks. The subordinates who evaluated Gunnar are a sales consultant and a marketing assistant. Gunnar's answers are a function of his personality, which he feels pretty good about, for the most part. He is not the type to standardize and discipline: he believes people need a certain degree of freedom and responsibility within their purview. That's the way he likes it best himself. However, that's not how his two coworkers see things. They think that it is a drawback that there are no clear agreements and limits for how time and resources should be spent, that requirements with respect to wording of market and sales materials, for example, are too lax, and – basically – that they need some guidelines for how to go about their day-to-day work. What they feel is necessary is something we can get out of them by talking with them, but it can also be revealed in a more systematic manner by using a questionnaire. The results from the systematic questionnaire approach can be seen in Figure 24, the gray profile. The profile outlined in gray shows that Gunnar should practice applying Blue and Gray leadership when needed, depending on the situation. Although he thinks it's boring, there is no doubt that he has to learn – and accept – that he has to go to the place where his employees are and lead them based on the needs they have and not from his own point of view and his needs. Comparing the profile outlined in gray with the one outlined in green, then, shows that he occasionally has to let go of Green and Red leadership. In the blue and gray corners you see the keywords representing the focus Gunnar needs to perform more in his leadership activities. But don't worry: Gunnar doesn't have to change his style or personality. What he needs to do is move his focus for a maximum total of two hours a week. That's all he has to do, and it is definitely neither impossible to learn nor impossible to do. So there you have it. Gunnar is an excellent leader by virtue of his personality, but he can become an even better one. How he can do that I will get to later when I introduce to you the Leader's Mental Scorecard.

Figure 24. An illustration of leadership focus moved to suit the situation at hand

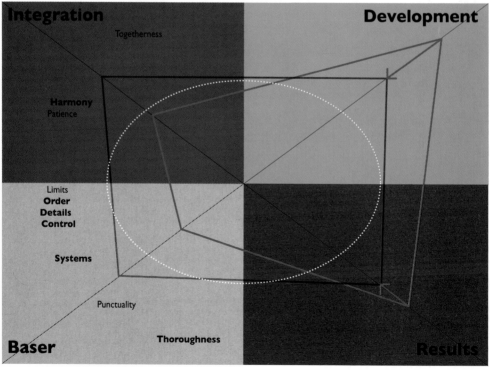

*The gray profile illustrates the change in focus Gunnar has to make to become a more successful leader.*

The Leader's Mental Scorecard. © Finn Havaleschka.

# V. The Leader's Mental Scorecard
## The Mental Handicap of Your Leadership

Please note that the profiles we present in this book contain no hidden assessment of whether these people are good or bad leaders. The profiles say nothing about whether they are able to put together leadership situation, focus and leadership style in the right way. Neither do the profiles say anything about whether the leaders behind the profile are, figuratively, able to move – mentally as well as in practice – from one focus area to another. However, to the extent you cannot do so, the idea behind this book is to learn. Figure 25 shows the profile of our Development leader once again.

## Figure 25. Profile of a Development leader with a Results focus

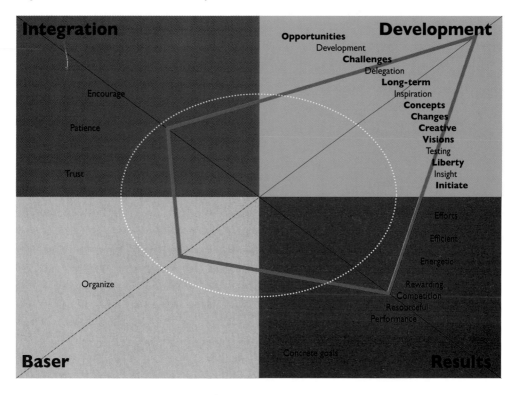

As you can see from the profile, this person has very little focus on Integration or Baser leadership. Most of this person's thinking and mental approach to leadership is Green. For him, leadership is about change, challenges, opportunity, creativity, visions, concepts, development, freedom, etc. – and also, to a certain extent, about Red leadership, i.e. focusing on performance, specific objectives, output and competition. What is completely or partly out of focus is Blue leadership, i.e. creating fellowship, understanding, harmony, agreement, showing consideration, being patient, helping, mediation and the like. Neither is there much focus on Gray leadership, which is the diagonal opposite of Green leadership. Gray leadership involves qualitative and practical elements such as control, checking, knowing details, setting limits, laying down rules, precision, security and accuracy.

We do not predict that this leader does not or is unable to focus on these elements of leadership, simply say that it is these things he has the least tendency to focus on and therefore most often overlooks or chooses not to make use of in his leadership. To the extent this is the case, then, the idea is to make him aware of the alternatives he is overlooking or ignoring and then help him develop the ability to practice these types of leadership. The Focus Model can be used as a starting point for creating this awareness (see Figure 26).

# Figure 26. The purpose behind the mental exercises

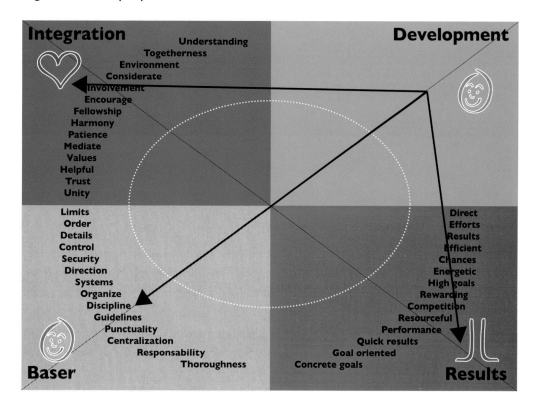

Figure 26 shows a leader who is located – figuratively, mentally and intellectually – in the Green corner. The arrows illustrate the directions in which this leader should also be able to move. Integration – showing understanding, being patient and considerate, etc. – has to do with feelings and empathy, which is why I put the heart of the Head-Heart-Legs[37] model in the Integration corner. Creating results and being energetic, efficient and goal-oriented have something to do with legwork – the ego – which is why I put the Legs in the Results corner of the model. Being focused on order, systematicism, rules and safety requires another intellectual and left-brained approach to things

---

[37] See the explanation of this model in footnote 34.

The Leader's Mental Scorecard. © Finn Havaleschka.

than this leader is used to taking, which is why I put the Head of the model down in the Baser corner.[38]

These symbols are intended to help create an awareness of where you need to move your focus. The next thing, then, is to figure out how to do it in practice. This is where the Leader's Mental Scorecard™ comes in. The Mental Scorecard contains a description of some practical leadership actions to be carried out in selected leadership situations, first mentally and then in reality.

As mentioned above, the Mental Scorecard idea is something I took from my efforts to introduce the concept of mental training for golfers. For those of you not familiar with the rules of the game, here is a brief description. When you play golf, you have a scorecard you use to keep a record of your score at each hole on the course. A hole is really a path to the hole that can be between 100 to 550 meters long. Each hole has an ideal score that depends on the length and difficulty of this path. If, for example the hole/path is 140 meters long, then the ideal score is to put the ball in the hole in three strokes. In other words, you get the ideal score if you can move the ball from the starting point into a hole only 8 cm in diameter that is 140 meters away, and you can do it hitting the ball only three times.

Normally, a golf course consists of 18 holes, i.e. 18 "paths" of different lengths. The whole idea is to hit your ball into all 18 holes in the fewest possible strokes. The more strokes (hits) you use above the ideal score for the entire course, the bigger your handicap. Normally, handicaps lie anywhere from plus 54 to minus 54. Only the very best players have a handicap above zero. The average handicap for the roughly 150,000 people in Denmark that play golf is minus 24; in other words, on a normal course they hit the ball 24 times more than is the ideal score for the course.

In the Leader's Mental Scorecard™, I have replaced the holes on the golf

---

[38] These symbols are there to help raise your awareness. When you think Integrator leadership, you think of focusing on and coming into contact with your Heart energy. When you think of Baser leadership, you think of the intellectual energy that expresses itself in logical left-brain thinking, i.e. your Head. When you think of Results leadership, you think of the Legs in the model, which symbolize moving ahead and the will to move, which is often motivated by your Head. To look at it figuratively, the person in Figure 26 needs to move his energy down to his legs. And to take the fourth component, when you think of Development leadership, you also think of intellectual energy, but this time creative right-brain thinking. Using this symbolization of the leadership areas or corners can help you to become aware more quickly of what is most important in the different leadership situations.

The Leader's Mental Scorecard. © Finn Havaleschka.

course with well-defined leadership actions, one leadership action corresponding to one hole on the golf course. But instead of playing a hole and then writing down your score, you carry out the leadership action described, first in your imagination and then in practice, and then write down your score, i.e. whether you were able to perform the action as you imagined it in your mind. If you succeed, you get two points; if not, you subtract two points. And this is how we calculate your leadership handicap. The closer to zero your handicap is, the closer you are to your ideal score, which – like your golf score –is an expression of your ability to carry out that particular leadership action.

Instead of the 18 holes that are always on a golfer's scorecard, a Leader's Mental Scorecard can contain a different number of actions, but normally up to six or seven. Another difference is that a golfer has to play the 18 holes all the way through in one run, while a manager using the Scorecard has 14 days to carry out the actions described on it.

The next parallel between the activities of golfers and leaders is the mental preparation of golfers. Most good golfers have some mental and physical routines they always go through before they hit the ball the first time at a hole, e.g. laying a strategy for how to play the hole and visualizing each stroke: where they want to hit the ball, in what kind of curve or straight, how high, etc. Next they make a couple of practice swings to loosen up tense muscles and to get the body ready to carry out the physical movement needed to hit the ball in a way that will put the ball where they want it.

The same is true of a person using the Leader's Mental Scorecard. With the Scorecard, before each situation in which you will practice taking a certain action, you lay out a strategy for how you will carry out that action. You imagine how you want to react and how you will carry out this action so the situation turns out the way you want it to. In this case, you must learn to follow the basic rule for mental training and behavior adjustment:

All other things being equal, what you do not imagine in advance and add to your psychological world, you will have difficulty carrying out in practice in the real world.

Diagram 3 shows a Mental Scorecard made for the Green leader we met above. How we make a scorecard and determine what leadership actions it should contain is something I will get back to later. Right now it is enough to know that the starting point in this case was this Green leader's own opinion of himself supplemented by the views of his superior, his colleagues and his subordinates. In other words, we obtained a 360-degree picture of this person first. To find the actions you should learn to carry out mentally and in practice, we use the statements about leadership focus in the questionnaire that you and other involved parties fill out. If, for example, you answered that you considered "formulating clear guidelines for subordinates' responsibilities and job performance" less important and the other people filling out the questionnaire agreed, but also felt that it would be a good thing for everyone if you attached greater importance to such activities, then you take that statement out of the questionnaire and put it in your Mental Scorecard, making it one of the actions you should practice to make yourself more aware of Gray leadership. See Diagram 1, where this statement has been written on the Scorecard as the first leadership action.

Your task now is to imagine in your mind how you would carry out the leadership action "formulating clear guidelines for subordinates' responsibilities and job performance, and ensuring that subordinates understand it." After this mental preparation, it is then up to you to find or create the situation or situations in which you can actually perform this action, setting yourself clear goals so you can make an assessment afterwards as to whether you achieved your goal or not.

The objective is to carry out this leadership action once or more during the next 14 days. Once the two weeks are up, you write down your score: two points if you think it went well; two points if it did not go well. Of course, you can ask other people for their opinions on that if you like: it may be a good idea to ask the person or persons you were practicing the leadership action on. You could also ask your own boss, or a mentor or coach, or a colleague who is also using the Leader's Mental Scorecard system.

Diagram 1 shows an example of this Mental Scorecard. The scorecard describes three types of situations or leadership actions intended to help this person become more aware of Gray leadership and thus better at implementing it. Next, it describes (1) two situations intended to help him focus more on certain elements of Red leadership and (2) two situations aimed at increasing his awareness of and ability to employ Blue leadership.

The Leader's Mental Scorecard. © Finn Havaleschka.

# Diagram 1. Mental Scorecard for the Green leader

| Sit· | Color | Focus, Calendar Weeks 17 and 18, 2004 | Points + | Points - |
|---|---|---|---|---|
| 1 | | **Action:** You need to formule clear guidelines for subordinates' responsibilities and work performance, and ensuring that they understand the guidelines | | |
| | | Evaluation: | | |
| 2 | | **Action:** Be aware that you make decisions based on clear and certain facts. | | |
| | | Evaluation: | | |
| 3 | | **Action:** Learn to control your reactions so you don't lose control of things. | | |
| | | Evaluation: | | |
| 4 | | **Action:** You need to set up specific goals for the work of each subordinate. | | |
| | | Evaluation: | | |
| 5 | | **Action:** Ensure that you and your subordinates utilize time and resources efficiently and in a targeted manner. | | |
| | | Evaluation: | | |
| 6 | | **Action:** Learn to involve coworkers in decisions so that no one feels left out. | | |
| | | Evaluation: | | |
| 7 | | **Action:** Try to create a shared understanding of what needs to be done and how, before you get the ball rolling. | | |
| | | Evaluation: | | |
| | | Results for the 14 days | | |
| | | **Ideal Score** (Number of actions x 2): | | |
| | | Your Mental Leadership Handicap | | |

This person worked with these leadership actions for 14 days, practicing them mentally and in actuality. With the help of a colleague, he devised a strategy for each action. First he carried out this action in his imagination, i.e. he tried to visualize how he would perform this action in reality, and visualize what kind of response he could expect to receive from different subordinates, the latter based on his own analysis of each person's personality-derived focus areas and thus their motivation and needs, and then he thought about what problems he might run into. Once this mental part of the process was in place, he found the place and time to carry out the action in practice. The Scorecard, Diagram 2, shows us how his first 14-day round went. Note his own evaluations under "**Evaluate your ability to focus on and carry out Gray leadership.**"

This leader's own comments and thinking give us food for thought and show that he has become more aware of how he can improve his own leadership. The first steps have been taken. He scored 6 out of a possible 14 points, which means his leadership handicap is 8. After the first round, he wipes the slate clean, so to speak, and starts a new round that plays itself out over the next 14 days. All the situations need to be acted out, also the ones he was good at the first time. Like a golfer, he keeps going, playing the Scorecard, until he brings his leadership handicap down to zero.

The Leader's Mental Scorecard. © Finn Havaleschka.

## Diagram 2. Mental Scorecard filled in by the Green leader

| Sit· | Color | Focus, Calendar Weeks 17 and 18, 2004 | Point + | Point - |
|---|---|---|---|---|
| 1 | | **Action:** You need to formule clear guidelines for subordinates' responsibilities and work performance, and ensuring that they understand the guidelines. | 2 | |
| | | *Evaluation: It's going all right, but I really need to get my act together.*<br>*Maybe I should only give myself one point.* | | |
| 2 | | **Action:** Be aware that you make decisions based on clear and certain facts. | | 2 |
| | | *Evaluation: Should learn to curb my enthusiasm before I start things up. Still having trouble with that.* | | |
| 3 | | **Action:** Learn to control your reactions so you don't lose control of things. | | 2 |
| | | *Evaluation:*<br>*Still get too emotionally involved and carried away.* | | |
| 4 | | **Action:** You need to set up specific goals for the work of each subordinate. | 2 | |
| | | *Evaluation:*<br>*I think it's going well!* | | |
| 5 | | **Action:** Ensure that you and your subordinates utilize time and resources efficiently and in a targeted manner. | | 2 |
| | | *Evaluation:*<br>*Probably still taking things too much for granted.* | | |
| 6 | | **Action:** Learn to involve coworkers in decisions so that no one feels left out. | | 2 |
| | | *Evaluation:*<br>*I need to do a lot more work on this!* | | |
| 7 | | **Action:** Try to create a shared understanding of what needs to be done and how, before you get the ball rolling. | 2 | |
| | | *Evaluation:*<br>*More practice and focus, and I'll get it right.* | | |
| | | Results for the 14 days | 6 | |
| | | **Ideal Score:** | 14 | |
| | | Your Mental Leadership Handicap | 8 | 8 |

*To see the scorecard on which this person and his coach wrote down the activities the former must carry out in his efforts to achieve the purpose of the leadership action.*

The Leader's Mental Scorecard. © Finn Havaleschka.

# Part One: Conclusion

After reading the above, you probably already have a pretty good idea what your own leadership style is. In the following, you will be filling in the questionnaire yourself and drawing your own profile. This will prove or disprove your own opinions on this subject. As stated before, however, the way you perceive yourself is one thing; another is how your subordinates, your colleagues and your boss see you. You will also have the opportunity to take a closer look at all this in the following, after taking photocopies of the questionnaires as instructed and asking others to fill them in for you. However, before you start, I would like to summarize the main points so far. The fundamental presumption is that your leadership style, your leadership behavior and what you focus on in your leadership – all of it is mainly determined by your personality, your temperament and your attitude to being a leader. Exactly for that reason, you often make your leadership decisions "in the absence of consciousness." Your leadership style – your way of viewing, tackling and dealing with problems – is a function of your personality, which is why people are often not especially aware of the spectrum of action that is actually available to them in a given situation. To make yourself aware of all the ways you can act in different situations, it is important that you improve:

- Your insight into your own leadership style, the one determined by your personality.
- Your awareness of how other people see you.
- Your ability to carry out a leadership process in your own imagination before you carry it out in real life.

One thing that can help you in this process of becoming more aware is the Focused Leadership Model, which divides leadership focus up into four qualities: Gray, Red, Blue and Green leadership. Once you know what your dominant leadership focus is and what area(s) you consciously or unconsciously do not focus so much on, then we put together a Mental Scorecard that lists some leadership actions you should perform, both mentally and in practice. The purpose of these actions is to increase your awareness of and ability to implement the type of leadership described. Next, on a more general level, you must become more aware of the factors that put a damper on your ability to determine, acknowledge and develop your inherent potential. In this connection, you must learn to be aware of the following and to act and make decisions:

- Independently of the good opinions of other people.
- Without any thought of gaining power over other people.
- Independently of the results of your efforts.[39]

If you are uncertain or in doubt as to whether a certain leadership action is appropriate or not, then the basic rule is that you must learn to put yourself smack dab in the middle of the Focus Model. From this figurative viewpoint, you can observe yourself and evaluate your own actions. Once you have made a choice, then look at what you think you will say or do and ask yourself, "Will it bring me peace of mind?" And remember, try not to waste your energy on something that you can't do anything about. In other words, don't worry. And if you do find that there really is something to worry about, and it is possible for you to do something to change things, then do it. But if you can't do anything about it, then there's no use worrying about it. With these principles as your mental guide, and with the Focused Leadership Model visualized in your imagination, you can now begin looking for answers to:

- Where are you (in the model)?
- What effect do you have on other people?
- Where are your subordinates (in the model)?
- How can you move from where you are to the places where your subordinates are?

---

[39] See p. 68 to make sure you do not misunderstand these sentences.

All of this you collect in one Mental Scorecard that puts together leadership situation, leadership focus and leadership style in the best possible way. You now have the materials, the tools and the opportunity, and the potential lies within you. Now it is your turn to set the course and run with it.

Let me conclude this part by quoting Rimpoche.

> We have to change our patterns of reacting to experience. For our problems do not lie in what we experience, but in the attitude we have towards it.[40]

---

[40] Akong Rimpoche. Quoted from *"I didn't want to be rich (just enough to re-upholster the couch)"*, Smallbone M. and Shilkin A., Thin Rich Press 1993, 52.

# Part Two
## Your Personal Starting Point

*The Four Basic Elements of Leadership - illustrations*

VI. Where Are You
   - *Know yourself and your reaction pattern*

VII. What Effect Do You Have on Others
   - *Your superior, your colleagues, your subordinates*

VIII. Where Are Your Subordinates
   - *The needs and personality of those under your leadership*

# Four Basic Elements of Leadership

Leadership can be divided into four different Focus areas. Each area is best served by one of the 4 types of personalities. The Baser, the Result, the Integrator and the Developer. It is very seldom that you will find a person who has the personality, interest and competence necessary to be able to serve all four areas successfully. This is why we have division of labor.

This is also the reason why we can identify four different types of crises, and four different approaches to crisis management. What becomes or is perceived as a crisis is very much dependent of the type of personality. What a Baser feels and perceives as a crisis, the Developer seldom considers a crisis. Just as what an Integrator perceives as a crisis, is seldom considered a crisis by the Result type.

In the following you will see the approach to management, what causes the feeling of a crisis and how the different types try to manage crises.

# Four Basic Focus Areas of Leadership

Leadership can be divided into 4 different Focus areas. Dependant of the position the leader holds, and the development and strategy of the organization, his job will likely require that he has more focus on one or two areas. How much a leader focuses on a given area is for the most part conditioned by the leader's personality as opposed to the situation and job requirement. *(Read the text from Baser to Result, to Integrator, to Developer focus).*

## ■ Integrator Focus

However the leader does not create the results by himself, but in cooperation with others. This naturally requires focus on the interaction and communication between people and their needs.

This is Integrator Focus.

*Leadership is about creating unity and being part of a community.*

## ■ Baser Focus

It is the leader's responsibility to organize and foresee the day-to-day activities.

This is Baser Focus.

*Leadership is about orderliness, creating structures and being in control.*

The Leader's Mental Scorecard. © Finn Havaleschka.

## Developer Focus ■

Finally the leader must take part in creating future results - which is Developer Focus.

*Leadership is about creating opportunities and being creative.*

## Result Focus ■

It is the leader's responsibility to create results, set up and achieve goals. This is Result Focus.

*Leadership is about creating results and reaching goals.*

The Leader's Mental Scorecard. © Finn Havaleschka.

# Four Basic Reasons for Managerial Crisis

The majority of leadership situations become crises as a result of the feelings brought about by the situation. Only then do we call it a crisis. We can distinguish between 4 different types of crises dependent of the type of personality. In this manner what may feel and be experienced as a crisis for one type of leader may not be so for another type. On these grounds we may tend to misunderstand, criticize or talk at crossed purposes. In reality this is usually the real reason that creates crisis.

## ■ Integrator crisis

For the Integrator Leader, not feeling part of the community will bring about crisis.

*The feeling of not being part of the community causes crisis.*

## ■ Baser crisis

For the Baser Leader it is situations of disorder and unpredictability that cause the feeling of not being in control, which leads to the experience of the situation being a crisis.

*The feeling of not being in control causes crisis.*

The Leader's Mental Scorecard. © Finn Havaleschka.

## Developer crisis ■

For the Developer Leader, it is the sense of limitation of opportunities for development that cause the feeling of crisis.

*The feeling of being restrained causes crisis.*

## Result crisis ■

For the Results Leader it is the sense of pending defeat that creates crisis.

*The feeling that you are going to lose causes crisis.*

The Leader's Mental Scorecard. © Finn Havaleschka.

# Four Basic Approaches to Crisis Management

When we experience that happiness is taken from us we guard ourselves - often by even more so of the same behavior that created the feeling of crisis to begin with. When cooperating to solve the "crisis" we therefore often stand in each our corner and move further into our corners - away from each other, the reason of and the solution to the conflict.

## ■ Integrator approach

The Integrator Leader will try even harder to avoid conflicts and to seek affirmation.

*Crisis management is avoiding conflicts.*

## ■ Baser approach

The Baser Leader will seek to solve the crisis with even more rules, structure and control over details.

*Crisis management is guarding against the unexpected.*

The Leader's Mental Scorecard. © Finn Havaleschka.

128

## Developer approach ■

The Developer Leader will try even harder to implement additional development projects and new ideas.

*Crisis management is being at the edge of development.*

## Result approach ■

The Results Leader seeks to solve the crisis with even more courage and by taking even more risks.

*Crisis management is having the guts to take a risk.*

The Leader's Mental Scorecard. © Finn Havaleschka.

# VI. Where are You

Know yourself and your reaction pattern

There are probably just as many perceptions of what leadership is and how it should be practiced as there are people, and there is nothing strange about that. Everything depends on the person and the situation. I'll spare you the learned discussion of the subject. On a practical but more general level, leadership is about setting goals and finding ways to achieve them, just as much as it is about evaluating and formulating the ethical and moral motives behind the goals and about the ways you intend to achieve the goals you have set. On a day-to-day operational level a leader's job is to create the best possible conditions for employees to do their work. To put it very simply, leaders provide a service. They are supposed to make it as easy as possible for their subordinates to do their jobs. In this respect leaders are Service Providers. Period. Once the objectives have been set and a reasonable degree of consensus on the ethical and moral motives behind the objectives has been obtained, then it is a question of finding the methods and means within this code of morals that are to be used to achieve the objectives. After this, it is a matter of division of labor, delegation of tasks and responsibilities – and providing service (leadership).

Good leadership strikes a balance between people. We are different; our knowledge, insight, status, salary, position, talents, educational backgrounds, attitudes, etc. vary, but we are all people who need to be understood, respected, accepted and appreciated. It is generally true that the greater the extent to which these needs are fulfilled, the more a person is willing to take responsibility and to apply his energy, creativity and capabilities to solving the tasks which have been delegated to him.

To create balance, a leader has to go to the place where his subordinate is, so to speak, and provide service to him or her from that place. And that is exactly what the Leader's Mental Scorecard is about. It starts with you

The Leader's Mental Scorecard. © Finn Havaleschka.

finding out where *you* are. To this end, you will be filling out a questionnaire and doing a number of different exercises, but before you start, I would ask you to consider the following.

## Your strength is also your weakness.

You are your personality. It's one thing none of us can run away from. Our personality is the only tool we have on the path towards fulfilling our ambitions in life. We have no other instruments; there is no quick fix on the road to happiness. We must learn to use the talents inherent in our personality as best we can. Sometimes, however, it seems as if our personality, in some situations, stands more in the way of the fulfillment of our ambitions than it helps us to fulfill them. Often we get to a point where it's difficult to keep on going. Our usual methods and attitudes, our usual behavior – none of it seems to take us any further – perhaps just the opposite. We can illustrate this fundamental rule using the four leadership types.

## Personal Qualities: From Strength to Weakness

### Baser Leaders:  From Thorough and Systematic to Restrictive and Controlling

Baser Leaders – technical, security-oriented, calculating and organized as they are – can reach a point where their strength turns into a weakness because their focus, their usual approach to people and things, blocks their ability to find alternative solutions. And that is how a Baser leader's strong side can become his weak one. You have probably seen similar situations yourself. Personally, I know someone who did an absolutely terrific job as a production manager and later as CEO for a small manufacturing company. In this first capacity, he was incredibly efficient, but when they made him CEO of a much bigger company, and direct contact with the production department constituted a smaller share of his activities, then everything went south. Just as he always did, everything had to be organized, structured, planned and checked. In the end, people at lower levels of the organization couldn't move for all the rules, limits, checks and control. Any flexibility or independence – and thus the will to take on responsibility – disappeared, and the structure and rules took over. The software we have developed at

*The Baser leader solving problems under pressure.*

Garuda in support of our coaching activities includes a model that, based on what a leader indicates in the questionnaire that he/she believes is more or less important, illustrates what happens to this leader's focus and thus to his/her pattern of actions when he/she feels pressured, i.e. when things don't go the way he/she intended, expected or hoped. It turns out that this simulation of behavior and reactions actually corresponds fairly well to reality. We can't put the computer model in this book, but I can show you on paper what typically happens with each type of leader. We will start with Figure 27, which shows the reaction typical of Baser leaders.

## Figure 27. The reactions of a Baser leader under pressure
(The bold profile)

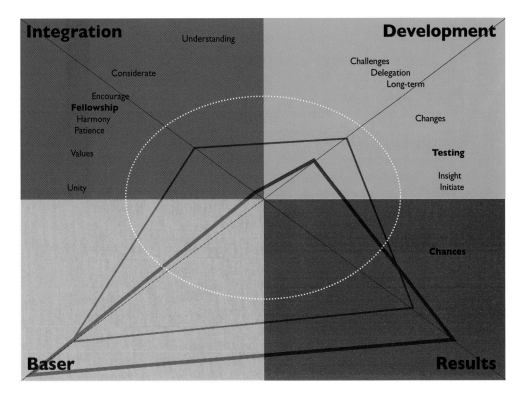

This person's normal focus is on Baser and Results leadership, and his highest score is in the Gray area, as you can see from his profile, drawn in the thin line. When this manager is under pressure, the profile outlined in a thick line illustrates the behavior and reaction pattern he will normally exhibit in this kind of situation: more control, more checking, and more pressure to get better results. So, he tends to apply discipline, control and orders, just like what actually occurred in the example above. Why does it happen? Why doesn't this person think to solve the crisis using methods from the other two areas of the Focus Model, or look for the cause of the crisis there? If, figuratively speaking, this Gray leader could put himself in the middle of the model, he would have an overview that would allow himself to ask why the crisis arose in the first place. Were his subordinates not motivated enough, not involved, or not informed well enough? Were there signals from his subordinates that could have warned him of a negative attitude or mood, signals that he did not pick up on? With this kind of overview, he could have moved into the Integrator area and asked some important questions about where the source of the pressure lies; then he could have found alternative solutions to the ones he usually chooses. Or he could have moved into the Green area and asked himself whether the crisis – this lack of motivation in his subordinates – could be due to them not having been given enough freedom. Maybe they felt so locked up by orders and rules that they couldn't come up with their own ideas or make independent decisions.

If this leader did not see or choose either of these two alternatives, then it is because he does not, under normal circumstances, have a focus on these areas. This can be clearly seen from the key words and phrases in his profile illustrated in figure 27, all of which have to do with the leadership actions he indicated in the questionnaire he did not feel were important. Patience, unity and understanding are elements of Integrator leadership that he has rejected, just as he has indicated that it was not important to give his subordinates the opportunity to participate in processes of change or throw themselves in to seek-and-learn processes. Perhaps the spotlight of his consciousness does occasionally land quite briefly on the Blue and Green areas of the model, but because he has not practiced trying to pick up or maintain a focus on – much less practice – these qualities, he cannot make use of them, especially not when he feels under pressure mentally, emotionally and/or physically.

## Results Leaders: From Persistent and Inspiring to Stubborn and Controlling

However, the fact that a strong side can become a weak one is not only true of Baser leaders. As highly results-oriented, persistent, direct and impatient as they are, Results leaders can also achieve their objectives to a certain point, but they are often stopped by those same qualities blocking their creativity, their ability to see other routes, and their ability to wait until the right time. And thus Results leaders' strength can become their weakness. I can use a story from my own experience to illustrate what I mean. Once, when I was a callow youth studying business, I participated in a panel debate together with top people from the Confederation of Danish Industries, Denmark's umbrella employers' organization. As a member of the panel, I had a great deal of opportunity to air my opinions and viewpoints and put forward my ideas. As was my habit, I became so absorbed in the subject and the discussion that several times I interrupted other people who were expressing their opinions. After the debate, we all went to the bar, and I was actually pretty well satisfied with myself and my performance, at least until one of the more experienced panel members pulled me to one side and, after complimenting me on my ideas, let drop a closing line: "Finn, you just need to be aware of one thing (at this point I prepared myself for flatter). You have a weakness: you ejaculate much too prematurely!" Now that was gender-specific educa-

*The Result leader solving problems under pressure.*

The Leader's Mental Scorecard. © Finn Havaleschka.

tion with a vengeance. Since then, I've probably gotten a bit better at modifying my behavior, but not much. The profile in Figure 28 is probably a fairly accurate representation of what my focus was back then. I hope that I have grown a bit wiser and a little more flexible over the years. However, the under-pressure profile, the one drawn in the thicker line, illustrates a behavior pattern that almost certainly excludes an empathic reaction, i.e. listening, being patient, carefully trying to sound out how others perceive your reactions and reasoning. Note that the under-pressure profile reaches a bit farther into the Gray and Green corners, but disappears entirely in the Blue area.

### Figure 28. The reaction pattern of a Results leader under pressure (The bold profile)

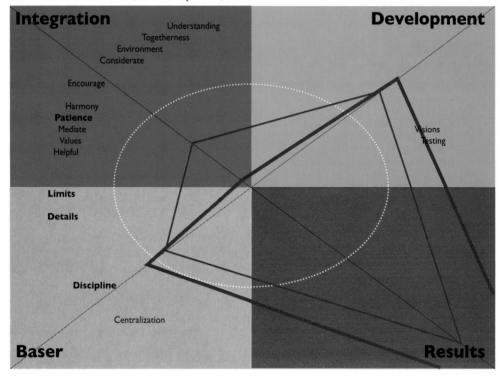

You probably recognize this pattern: if not from yourself, then from other people. When they are under pressure, people with this kind of profile don't listen or try to understand or find alternative points of view; they repeat, in a kind of variation on a theme, the same reasoning again and again, in a louder and louder voice. They shout a little more loudly and run a little faster in an attempt to get somewhere, but they don't solve their problem; they dig themselves deeper into it. If you recognize this pattern in yourself, then the next time it happens, try to move up into the Blue corner. It is difficult at first, but you can learn to do it.

## Integrator Leaders: From Attentive and Involved to Conflict-Shy and Passive

In many ways the opposite of Results leaders, Integrator Leaders attach importance to living up to other people's expectations so they don't disappoint others or push them away. They also try to avoid conflict, seek harmony and understanding, and want to make sure everyone is on board and happy to be there. However, they can also reach a certain point where their motivating drive turns into a weakness, when they don't make choices that are in accordance with their inner nature: to say what they really believe and do what they feel deep down inside is right. In that way, the strong side of Integrator leaders can be their weak side as well. In all areas of life, there are situations when we have to choose to do or do without. As a leader, you have to be willing to go against the flow, not just to be contrary, but contrary to what others

*The Integrator leader solving problems under pressure.*

The Leader's Mental Scorecard. © Finn Havaleschka.

do. If you aren't, you risk things falling apart. There is no doubt that leaders who have a strong Integrator focus are best when things are going their way. When the wind is at your back, it is easy to satisfy other people and be friends with everyone, but what happens when the wind changes direction and you have to make less pleasant decisions? The profile of an Integrator leader under pressure in Figure 29 provides a very clear and realistic illustration of what this person's "normal" reaction pattern is.

Figure 29. The reaction pattern of an Integrator leader under pressure (The bold profile)

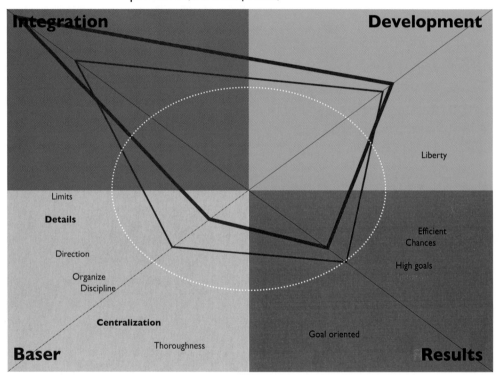

When they are under pressure, Integrator leaders tend to let go of the reins, attaching even less importance to discipline and having people remain within the given framework and rules; they move away from Gray and Red leadership in order to strengthen their mediating, accommodating and understanding behavior. They do not insist or take command, and this reduces their chances of solving the problem.

### Development Leaders: From Creativity and Vision to Fantasies and Chaos

Fourth but not least, we have Development leaders, who are creative and visionary. They seek change, they like to experiment, and they thrive in complexity and chaos. However, these qualities, too, may sooner or later turn into a weakness due to a lack of structure, order, practical substance and pragmatism. Thus the strong side of Development leaders is also their weak side.

*The Developer leader solving problems under pressure.*

As can be seen in Figure 30, this Green leader usually becomes more Green and more Red when he is under pressure because things aren't going the way they should. He experiments more, tries out more creative ideas, wants more freedom, etc. That it might be a lack of discipline or attention to detail and a disorganized, unsystematic way of working that is the root cause for the crisis is not something that occurs to this Green leader at all. As a result, neither does it occur to him that this kind of approach to the problem might just be the solution.

## Figure 30. The reaction pattern of a Development leader under pressure (The bold profile)

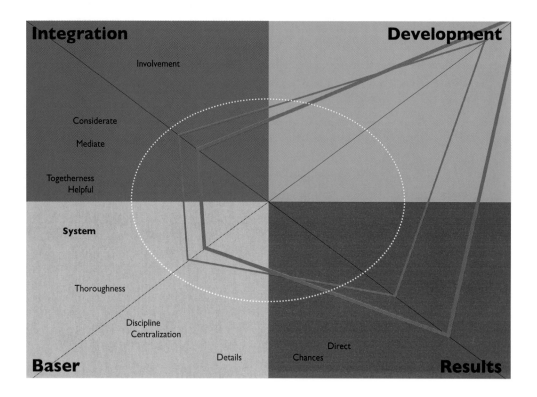

## The Sweet Spot of the Personality

My conclusion is that we must learn to acknowledge the weakness in the strength and the strength in the weakness before we can learn to exploit the full potential that lies in our personality. We have to learn to sit down in the middle of the model, and from this point of view then evaluate what kind of leadership the current situation requires. In principle, you could say that we need to learn to neutralize our deeply rooted habits, move ourselves into the middle, and then move out from there into the type of leadership that is best suited to the situation. This philosophy can be illustrated by the following model. Figure 31.

# Figure 31. The Sweet Spot of the personality
(Place yourself at the center and follow the needs of the situation
- not your own)

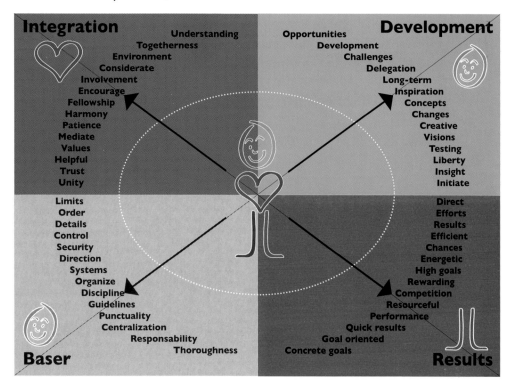

When you hit a golf ball with complete precision, it's called hitting the ball's Sweet Spot. If you ever played soccer, it's the same feeling you get when you hit the ball just right with your foot. It feels like you can make the ball move very precisely where you want it and very fast without trouble and without expending a lot of energy. The same thing happens when you use the right kind of leadership to get things running like a well-oiled machine. This is what happens when your leadership is based on your personality's Sweet Spot: the place where your personality is wholly in balance and you can move around from one leadership style to another in all four areas with ease. The purpose of the following exercises is to help you find your personal – or should we call it your leadership – Sweet Spot.

## Find a Development Partner

To get the maximum benefit from these exercises, I recommend you find a partner or coach that can help you with these tests, evaluations and exercises. It may be a good idea to find a partner, friend or colleague who is also working with these same methods and exercises. Of course, it is completely up to you how much work you want to put into the exercises described below. The most important thing is for you to get a clear picture of your own focus, your own behavior and the values and attitudes behind it, and learn to see them so clearly that you are always able to consider their advantages and disadvantages in different situations and with different people.

## Draw Your Profile

The questionnaire you are about to fill out is intended to function as a starting point for you to think about what you think is important – and not so important – in your day-to-day work as a manager of other people. Document 1, a questionnaire[42], is at the back of this book. Once you've filled out this questionnaire and calculated your score using Document 2, then draw your Leader Profile in Figure 32. The diagram in Figure 32 can also be found at the back of the book, entitled Document 3. Now fill in your questionnaire and plot your profile below.

## Figure 32. Your Leadership Profile

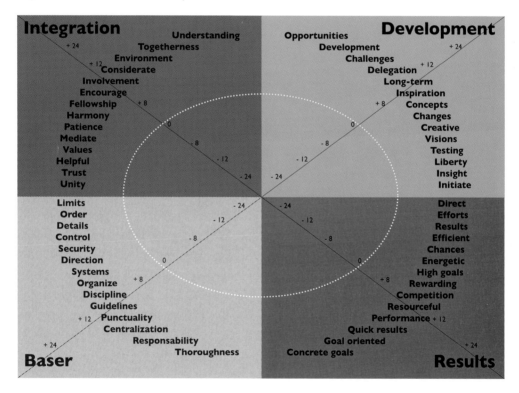

---

42  Forms and questionnaire sheets to be filled in and for photocopying are in the appendix at the back of the book, and they are called "Document 1", "Document 2", etc. If I refer to a figure, diagram, etc. that is not at the back of the book, then it will not be called a document, but Figure 1 or Diagram 2, for example.

The Leader's Mental Scorecard. © Finn Havaleschka.

*Exercise 1*

## Describing your leadership focus

What I want you to do now is to describe your leadership focus. At the back of the book, you will find general descriptions of each of the four types of leadership. We operate with "Main Type" descriptions (Document 4), "Selected Type" descriptions (Document 5), and "Deselected Type" descriptions (Document 6). Your Main Type is the focus area in which you obtained the largest number of points. If, for example, you obtained the largest number of points in the Integrator area, then you should find the description in the "Integrator Leader" box under **Main Type Descriptions**. Next, you should find your Selected Type and Deselected Type descriptions. The focus area in which you received the next-highest score is your Selected Type, and the area in which you received the lowest score (less than four points) is your Deselected Type.

Please note that these descriptions have only one purpose: to serve as inspiration and to get you thinking about and discussing your approach to leadership. The descriptions alone have no truth value: their truth value lies in the discussion that they are intended to inspire, and not in the descriptions themselves.

Figure 33 shows a profile I made to help guide you in how to put together your own description.

The highest number of points this person scored (24) is in the Development area, so the description of the **Development leader** under the "Main Type Description" heading in Document 4 will contain the description most relevant for the person being profiled. The second-highest number of points (12) is in the Results area, which means we go in under "Selected Type Descriptions" in Document 5 and find the box with that contains "**Selection of the Results role**" (the red box). Lastly, this person 's profile has the lowest number of points (minus 7) in the Baser field, which leads to the box in Document 6 in which we find "**Deselection of the Baser role**" (the gray

# Figure 33. An example of a leadership profile

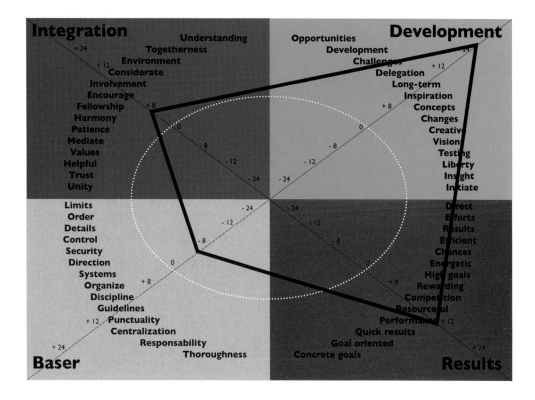

The Leader's Mental Scorecard. © Finn Havaleschka.

box). In general, if your score is around zero, i.e. between minus three and plus three, then this means you have selected some and deselected others of the statements within the focus area in question. As a result, none of the descriptions will be especially accurate ones of your leadership style as you practice it. This does not mean that you cannot read these descriptions anyway and get something out of them; it simply means that not everything in the descriptions will be something you see in yourself. However, if we look again at the profile above and follow the instructions, the following passages will be relevant.

**Development leaders** want to be out ahead of the pack; work with long-term perspectives; develop general concepts and strategies, visions and ideas; find creative solutions; and test, discuss and experiment with new opportunities.

Normally, Development leaders feel it is extremely important to inspire and encourage their subordinates to take on challenges and to be proactive and forward-looking. This also means that subordinates have a considerable degree of freedom and room to try out their own ideas and make independent decisions.

Change, creative solutions, new opportunities, concepts, visions, long-term goals, experiments, freedom, entrustment and independence are thus key words in describing the approach Development leaders take to their role as a manager.

A disadvantage of this approach to management may be that the subordinates lack limits and more specific and short-term objectives to aim for. Focusing on visions, new concepts and ideas can, for some workers, lead to insecurity in their everyday work life. Change – both real change and change only talked about – happens too quickly for some people, and this can make some workers feel insecure about their future, their place, and what they will be doing tomorrow.

**Selection of the Results role** may also mean that subordinates easily feel pressured because great demands – perhaps impossible ones – are made on them in their daily work.

One consequence may be workers who feel stressed and dissatisfied who do not feel that they are being listened to, or that no consideration is shown to individual worker competencies and desires.

**Deselection of the Integrator role** may mean that subordinates go their own way and pursue their own goals without showing consideration toward other people because there is no sense of fellowship and thus no feeling of responsibility toward others and the group. In such circumstances, there is no motivation to help others, and in the worst-case scenario, each worker or group isolates themselves, which again may lay the foundation for conflict and poor teamwork.

The Leader's Mental Scorecard. © Finn Havaleschka.

Now take your own profile and put together your own description. Take a copy of the descriptions at the back of the book in Documents 4, 5 and 6. Cut out the relevant descriptions and paste them onto an ordinary piece of A4-format paper. If you want to and have the equipment, you can scan them into a Word document and cut and paste there. However you do it, the most important thing is to collect your descriptions into a document that you can use as a starting point for your work. Now discuss the descriptions with your coach. You can use the following questions as a guide:

- Do the descriptions depict your leadership style?
- In what connections do you or you and your coach see your strong and weak sides?
- In what situations?
- When working with which subordinates?
- Does your focus suit the tasks, people and areas of responsibility you are supposed to be managing?
- What are your strong and weak sides?
- Is there anything you would like to improve on?

In the following, I have outlined a few exercises you can do to help you gain a clearer insight into your leadership style. After you discuss the above with your coach, you will be ready to begin upon the following exercises.

Find some of the phrases in the paragraphs you have just cut and pasted together that you think best describe your strong sides as a leader. Write them down on the left side of Diagram 4. On the right side, write what you think are the advantages of the behavior you described on the left.

To give you an example, on the left side of the diagram below, I wrote "*inspire and encourage coworkers to be proactive and forward-looking.*" I took this wording from my own Main Type description. Below is what I cut out from my Main Type description.

**Development leaders** want to be out ahead of the pack; work with long-term perspectives; develop general concepts and strategies, visions and ideas; find creative solutions; and test, discuss and experiment with new opportunities.

Normally, Development leaders feel it is extremely important to inspire and encourage their subordinates to take on challenges and to **be proactive and forward-looking**. This also means that subordinates have...

Next, on the right side I wrote down the advantages that I believe that my leader style "inspiring and encouraging my subordinates to take on challenges and to be proactive and forward-looking" has for my subordinates. Now you do the same thing, using Diagrams 3 and 4 to make your notes in.

## Diagram 3. Listing the advantages of your focus

| Strong/good sides (words, phrases or concepts) you found in your Main Type description | Advantages for you and your subordinates |
|---|---|
| **Example:** *Encouraging subordinates to be proactive and forward-looking.* | **Example:** *Working with new things, initiating things, setting the course. Subordinates have more freedom and challenges!* |
| **Strong sides:** | **Advantages:** |

On the left-hand side of Diagram 4, next page, write the same things you did in Diagram 3, and then think about and list the disadvantages that can also be associated with the behavior described.

## Diagram 4. Listing the disadvantages of your focus

| Strong/good sides (words, phrases or concepts) you found in your Main Type description<br><br>*Example:* Encouraging coworkers to be proactive and forward-looking | Disadvantages for you and your subordinates<br><br>*Example:* Maybe I don't go into enough detail myself. Maybe asking too much of some people, and some people may need more precise instructions. |
| --- | --- |
| **Strong sides:** | **Disadvantages:** |

 *Exercise 3*

Go back to the first questionnaire you filled in at the back of the book (Document 1). I suggest you take a copy of it to make it easier for you to do this exercise. Then find four of the statements in the questionnaire that you indicated were **A lot** and write them down in Diagram 5, one statement each in columns 1 to 4. Then list at least ONE situation from your everyday work life in which the focus described was an advantage. Next, find *one* situation in which the focus described was inappropriate or counterproductive.

# Diagram 5. Advantages and disadvantages of a focus

| | *In my daily decisions and in my role as a leader, I believe the following is:* | *A lot* |
|---|---|---|
| *Example* | Write a statement from questionnaire:<br>*Making my decisions based on clear and certain facts* | |
| | Example of an advantage: *We minimize errors; we seldom have to do things a second time; and we always know where we are.* | |
| | Example of a disadvantage: *Maybe things go too slow once in a while; we don't take any chances.* | |
| 1 | A statement from Document 1 to which your response was **A lot**: | |
| | Describe a situation in which it would be an advantage. | |
| | Describe a situation in which it would be a disadvantage. | |
| 2 | A statement from Document 1 to which your response was **A lot**: | |
| | Describe a situation in which it would be an advantage. | |
| | Describe a situation in which it would be a disadvantage. | |
| 3 | A statement from Document 1 to which your response was **A lot**: | |
| | Describe a situation in which it would be an advantage. | |
| | Describe a situation in which it would be a disadvantage. | |
| 4 | A statement from Document 1 to which your response was **A lot**: | |
| | Describe a situation in which it would be an advantage. | |
| | Describe a situation in which it would be a disadvantage. | |

 *Exercise 4*

## Advantages and disadvantages of the absence of a type of leadership focus

Go back to the questionnaire in Document 1 again. Find four statements to which you answered *Not much* or *Not at all*. Write them down in Diagram 6. Now describe at least *one* situation in which your focus (or, rather, your lack of focus) was an advantage. Next, find *one* situation in which the lack of focus in this area caused problems.

## Diagram 6. Advantages and disadvantages of absence of focus

| | *In my daily decisions and in my role as a leader, I believe the following is:* | *Not at all* |
|---|---|---|
| **1** | Write a statement from Document 1 to which your response was **Not at all**: | |
| | Describe a situation in which the absence of focus was an advantage. | |
| | Describe a situation in which it would be a disadvantage. | |
| **2** | Write another statement from Document 1 to which your response was **Not at all**: | |
| | Describe a situation in which it would be an advantage. | |
| | Describe a situation in which it would be a disadvantage. | |
| **3** | Write another statement from Document 1 to which your response was **Not at all**: | |
| | Describe a situation in which it would be an advantage. | |
| | Describe a situation in which it would be a disadvantage. | |
| **4** | Write another statement from Document 1 to which your response was **Not at all**: | |
| | Describe a situation in which it would be an advantage. | |
| | Describe a situation in which it would be a disadvantage. | |

## What you dislike about other types

Now I want you to take a look at what you don't like about other types of people, both leaders and subordinates. There are a number of concepts listed in the focus model in Figure 34, each of which represents a certain type of behavior and a few attitudes and values. Find and underline six of the words, phrases or concepts that best represent the people, behavior, attitudes and values that you have the hardest time accepting, maintaining a positive attitude towards, and thus working together with.

## Figure 34. The Focus Model

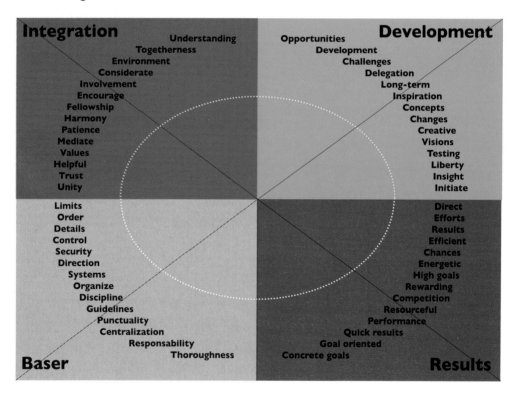

Once you have done that, then write again, in Diagram 7, what you underlined, then describe the disadvantages you see in the resultant behavior. Write down also, if you can, the situations you can think of in which you did not find this behavior to be optimal in the given situation or where you think it was obstructive or irritating. Then discuss your opinions and attitudes with your coach.

## Diagram 7. Disadvantages of focus behavior

| Concept | Concept from Figure 34 | **Disadvantages** of the resultant behavior |
|---|---|---|
| Example | Example: Details | e.g. in the following situation: In the follow-up at product meetings: *We come to a standstill, and spend time checking unnecessarily* |
| 1 | Concept: | e.g. in the following situation: |
| 2 | Concept: | e.g. in the following situation: |
| 3 | Concept: | e.g. in the following situation: |
| 4 | Concept: | e.g. in the following situation: |
| 5 | Concept: | e.g. in the following situation: |
| 6 | Concept: | e.g. in the following situation: |

Now do the same thing, just in the reverse polarity, so to speak. Take the same six words, phrases or concepts, and this time describe the advantages that this kind of behavior can also entail.

## Diagram 8. Advantages of the behavior

| Concept | Concept form figure 34 | **Advantages** of the resultant behavior |
|---|---|---|
| Example | Concept: *Details* | eg. in the following situation: *In production planning: We have things under control; we don't waste time on surprises.* |
| 1 | Concept: | Advantages:<br><br>e.g. in the following situation: |
| 2 | Concept: | Advantages:<br><br>e.g. in the following situation: |
| 3 | Concept: | Advantages:<br><br>e.g. in the following situation: |
| 4 | Concept: | Advantages:<br><br>e.g. in the following situation: |
| 5 | Concept: | Advantages:<br><br>e.g. in the following situation: |

## General advantages and disadvantages of the four leadership styles

Now, in the same way, try to name the overall advantages and disadvantages you see in each of the four types of leadership. As much as you can, ignore your own preferences and simply focus, intellectually and analytically, on the effect that each type of leadership has. See the example given in Diagram 9.

When I look at the concepts in the Baser area, I see some advantages too, for example, order, control, verification and responsibility. So I write down these advantages in the diagram under "Advantages of Baser Leadership." However, I can also see some disadvantages, which I then list under "Disadvantages of Baser Leadership." I can see advantages and disadvantages of all the other concepts as well. The ones mentioned are intended as examples.

## Diagram 9. Advantages and disadvantages of Baser leadership

| Advantages of Baser Leadership: | |
| --- | --- |
| With **Order**, you avoid surprises and wasted time.<br>With **Control**, we always know where we are.<br>**Guidlines** ensures the quality promised.<br>Assigning **Responsibility** lets people know what they are supposed to do. | |
| 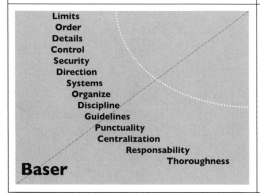 | **Disadvantages of Baser Leadership:**<br><br>**Order.** Too much wasted time.<br>**Control.** Tight control hampers new initiatives.<br>**Guidlines:** Irritates workers and gives rise to distrust.<br>**Responsibility.** Detailed assignment of responsibilities inhibits people's desire to take on a wider range of responsibility. |

Now do the same for all four leadership types. Use Diagrams 10 to 13. When you are finished, then discuss your results with your development partner.

## Diagram 10. Advantages and disadvantages of Baser leadership

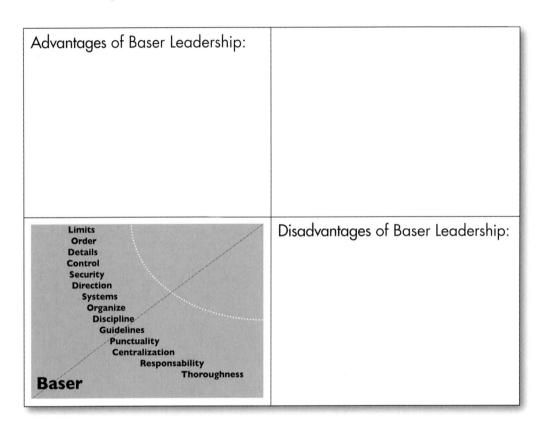

Advantages of Baser Leadership:

Limits
Order
Details
Control
Security
Direction
Systems
Organize
Discipline
Guidelines
Punctuality
Centralization
Responsability
Thoroughness

**Baser**

Disadvantages of Baser Leadership:

# Diagram 11. Advantages and disadvantages of Results leadership

|  | Advantages of Results Leadership |
|---|---|
| Disadvantages of Results Leadership | |

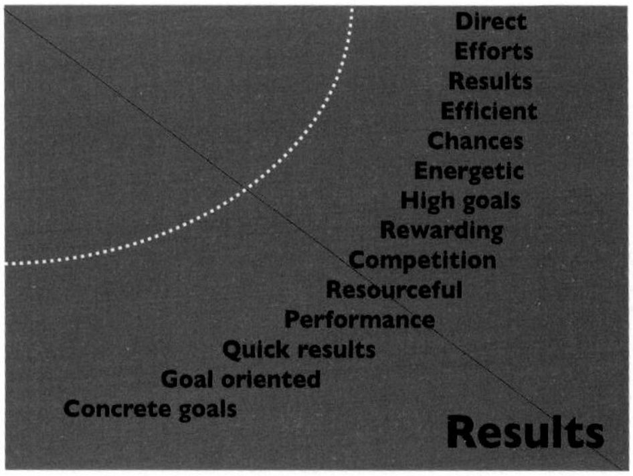

Diagram 12. Advantages and disadvantages of Integrator leadership

| | |
|---|---|
| 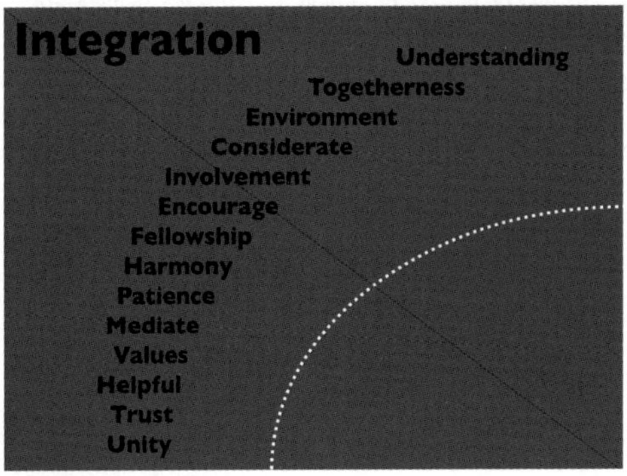 **Integration** Understanding Togetherness Environment Considerate Involvement Encourage Fellowship Harmony Patience Mediate Values Helpful Trust Unity | Advantages of Integrator Leadership |
| Disadvantages of Integrator Leadership | |

Diagram 13. Advantages and disadvantages of Development
            leadership

| Advantages of Development Leadership: | |
|---|---|
| | Disadvantages of Development Leadership: |

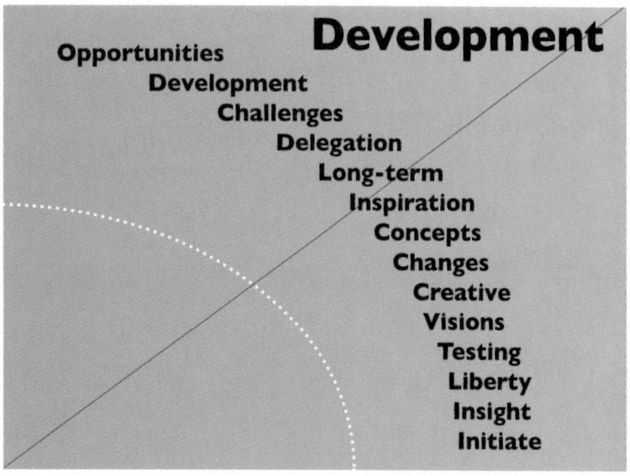

To conclude, I would ask you and your coach to think a bit about the following statements. These sentences were taken from Part One of this book. If you are in doubt about how you should understand these statements, then go back to Part One of the book.

**We want to stay where we feel safest and most secure.  Page 66.**
- For example, in which leadership situations do you feel most secure?
- What is it that makes you feel secure?
- In which leadership situations do you experience the greatest happiness or satisfaction?
- What is it that makes you feel happy?

**What you see depends on where you stand.  Page 82.**
- For example, can you think of situations in which your own assessment or behavior has been colored by your way of looking at things – what you feel most secure with or what brings you the greatest happiness?
- Can you find situations in which your assessment or behavior has been colored by the opposite: what makes you feel insecure or uneasy?

**You have to dare to lose your foothold to move forward. Page 68.**
- Can you think of situations in which your strong sides turned into weak sides because you were afraid of losing your foothold?

**Sometimes we have to let go so that we can hold on. Page 89.**
- Can you think of situations in which you held onto your usual behavior and attitudes and got the opposite of what you wanted?

# VIII. What Effect Do You Have on Others

## Your superior, your colleagues, your subordinates

One of the most difficult and frustrating things in life is trying to find out how other people see you. People are not going to see you from your point of view, but from their own. You can try to get closer to a person, which will probably change this person's view of you, if that's what you want, but you can't force this person to come over and stand where you are and see you from your own point of view.

One thing is what you say; how other people hear what you say is quite another. It is unequivocally true that:

> Before other people tune into what you are saying or your ideas, they tune into your aura.

Some people are highly conscious of their charm and the way other people perceive and react to it; other people don't think so much about it. Unfortunately, I have no questionnaires about radiation and its ffect on other people's perceptions, but we can make a type of so-called "360-degree analysis" I call Mirror Profiles. What we use are questionnaires with the same questions you answered yourself, but instead we ask other people to answer based on how they see you. Since the questions are the same as the ones you answered (with small changes to the sentence structure), we can then compare your perception of yourself with how others perceive you. See figure 35.

## Figure 35. The 360-degree feedback model

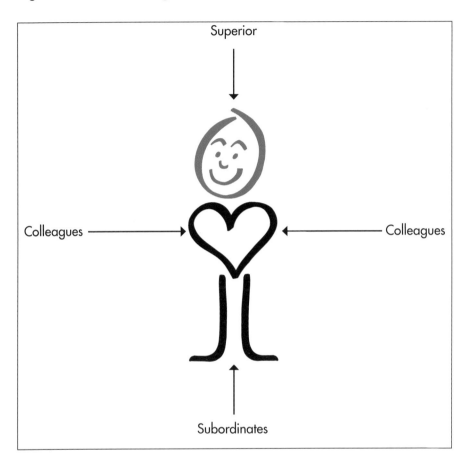

At the back of the book, you will find questionnaires you can photocopy and ask your boss (Document 7), some of your colleagues (Document 8), and your subordinates (Document 9) to fill in. In principle, there are no limits on how many colleagues and subordinates can fill out a Mirror Profile. That's up to you. The most important thing is that you don't **only** ask people you have a good relationship with to give you feedback. It is vital that you also receive feedback from people that you might not get along with quite so well.

Take as many copies as you need from the questionnaires at the back of the book and give them to the people you would like to have feedback from. Show them the Focus Model and tell them a bit about the purpose behind it. If you have subordinates who would like to help you but wish to remain anonymous, then you can let your coach handle it and have him guarantee their anonymity. Anonymity can be important if you want detailed and realistic feedback; on the other hand, it means you won't be able to talk with these people directly.

Once you have received the questionnaires back, then you convert them into profiles in graphical form. For instructions on how to do this, see the instructions at the back of the book (Document 10). When you plot the profiles, you can draw one profile on each sheet (Document 11) if you wish, but it is easier to compare them if you draw all your colleague's Mirror Profiles on one sheet – using different-colored lines, for example –and those of your subordinates on another.

From experience, we know that you begin to get an idea of how other people see you when you tally your scores (i.e. count the points for each of the questionnaires). This can give you a lot of "aha" experiences, but also many surprises – which is the idea. Once you have drawn the profiles, we have suggestions below about how to systematically work out and describe your immediate impressions in words, images and situations.

Draw the Mirror Profiles onto the Focus Models in Figures 36 to 38.

Figure 36. How your superior perceives your leadership behavior

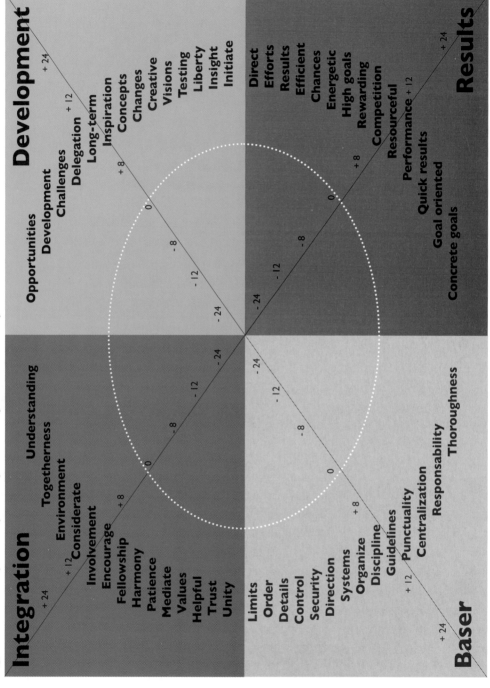

Figure 37. How your colleagues perceive your leadership behavior

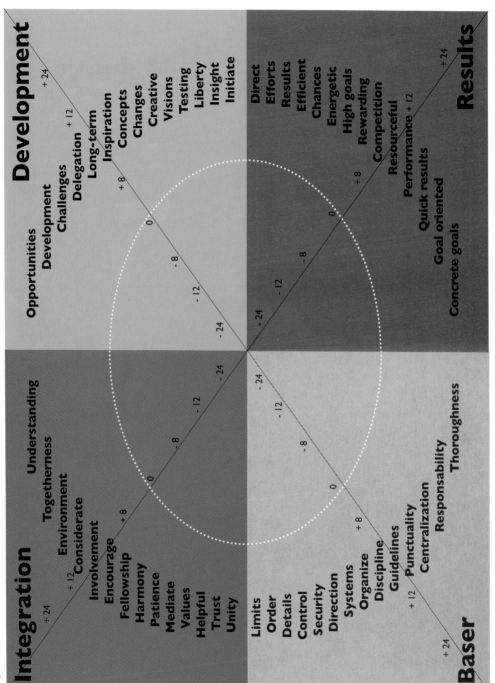

Figure 38. How your subordinates perceive your leadership behavior

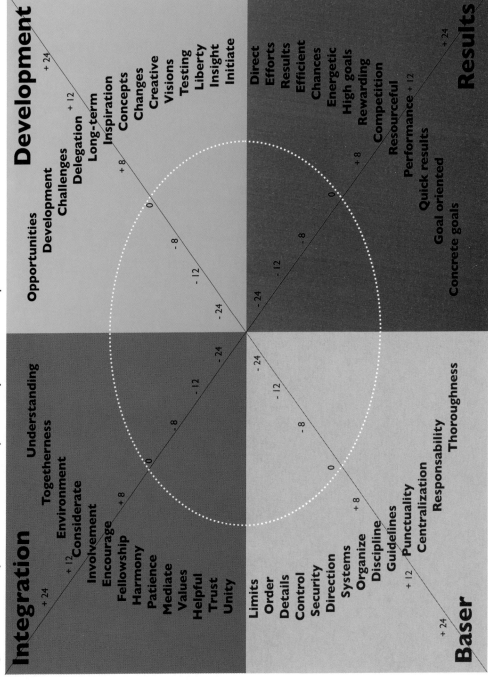

The Leader's Mental Scorecard. © Finn Havaleschka.

## Describing How Other People See Your Leadership Focus

Now it is time for you to put together a description of how other people perceive you as a leader, and you should do it in the same way as you did when you put together the description of your own profile. The descriptions and instructions are at the back of the book. It is up to you whether or not you put together a separate description for each person who gives you feedback. Generally, of course, if the profiles look like each other in their graphical representation, then the written descriptions will also be similar. The more the various perceptions of your leadership style differ, the more reason you have to draw and put together a description for each Mirror Profile. As with your own profile, it is best to cut and paste the relevant descriptions together. The most important thing is for you to put together a document that is easy for you to use in the work ahead.

Please note – again – that these descriptions only have one purpose: to serve as inspiration and to get you started on thinking and discussing your approach to leadership as others see it. The descriptions themselves have no truth value. Truth value can only be found in the discussion that the descriptions inspire, not in the descriptions themselves.

 *Exercise 7*

## Looking at other people's perceptions of your leadership focus

The first thing you should do now is look at the descriptions you put together and think about how other people see you. As much as you can, try to look at these descriptions objectively: don't think about whether other people have the right or wrong perception or think well or badly of you. Try to remain completely neutral while you are reading the descriptions. Then begin thinking about why you are perceived in the way you are.

First, together with your coach, consider your relationship with your superior. Here are a number of questions to help you do just that.

The Leader's Mental Scorecard. © Finn Havaleschka.

- What kind of relationship do you have with your boss?
- Do you, in your opinion, have a good working relationship?
- Do you normally understand each other– right away?
- What kind of expectations, generally, do you think your boss has to you?
- To what extent do you think you live up to your boss' expectations?
- Do you think his/her expectations are relevant?
- In what areas, if any, do you two have different perceptions of things?
- Do these different perceptions give rise to friction in the workplace?

Next, consider your relationships with your colleagues and then your subordinates, and ask yourself the same questions. First go through all this with your development partner. Don't discuss the feedback with the person providing it until you have discussed it with your partner. Exercise 8 explains how to talk with others about their view of you.

 *Exercise 8*

## Discussing other peoples' views of your leadership focus

The next step is to meet with your boss and then with your colleagues and subordinates. Start by telling them about the Focus Model and the philosophy behind it:

- Explain a bit about the four focus areas using the key words in the model shown in Documents 12 or 13 at the back of the book.
- Explain how you draw a Mirror Profile and stress that the model as such has no value: by itself, a profile is neither good nor bad. Everything depends on the leadership situation and the ability of the person being profiled to figuratively move around inside the model to find the best focus for the situation and person in question.
- Next have a free discussion of how this person sees your leadership focus.
- Take the graphical profile that shows your own view of your leadership focus and compare it with the Mirror Profiles. Discuss similarities and differences.

After a run-through of the key words and the graphical profiles, you can go into greater detail. You do that by taking the questionnaire that the person you are interviewing filled in and going through each of the 24 statements that person responded to. Make sure you have a copy of your own questionnaire at hand so that you can find and discuss especially those statements to which the two of you had different responses.

This process can be very rewarding, instructive, validating and uplifting, but also a little tough and frustrating. You risk hearing the kind of thing no one much likes to hear. However, do remember that this is about learning to go to the place where the other person is and meet him/her there. To repeat what I said above, at the start of this section of the book:

*"People are not going to see you from your point of view, but from their own. You can try to get closer to a person, which will probably change this person's view of you, if that's what you want, but you can't force this person to come over and stand where you are and see you from your own point of view".*

So don't expect other people to come to you. It is your job to go to them, to understand their thought processes and their point of view.

## Perceptions Based on Different Values or Attitudes

Once you have held these interviews as suggested, you must try to rise above and liberate yourself from the more subjective feelings that these discussions may have brought about. In the Focus Model in Figure 34, I put a brief description in each focus area. The description in the Red area, the Result leader's area, briefly depicts how a Red leader sees him/herself: as an energetic, active and goal-oriented leader. However, the question is also how this person is perceived by others. In principle and in practice, it could well be that other people also see the Red leader as energetic, active and goal-oriented; i.e. that the Mirror Profiles other people return to this individual are identical to the profile he/she made of him/herself. However, behind this same evaluation there may be different underlying values and attitudes, likes and/or dislikes. In the example with Gunnar in the first part of this book, we saw that Gunnar's coworkers saw his focus exactly the same way he saw it himself, but we also observed that there were a few things with respect to Blue and Gray leadership that they thought Gunnar should have a little bit more focus on.

Perhaps you also see yourself as energetic, active and goal-oriented. It is you, your personality, that you feel good about – that you think is positive. But how is this behavior perceived subjectively by someone whose primary focus is on Blue activities, for example? In Figure 39, I wrote in the Integrator area, *"A Blue person sees a Red leader as an impatient, brash and perhaps slightly inconsiderate leader."*

Figure 39. How a Red leader is perceived by others

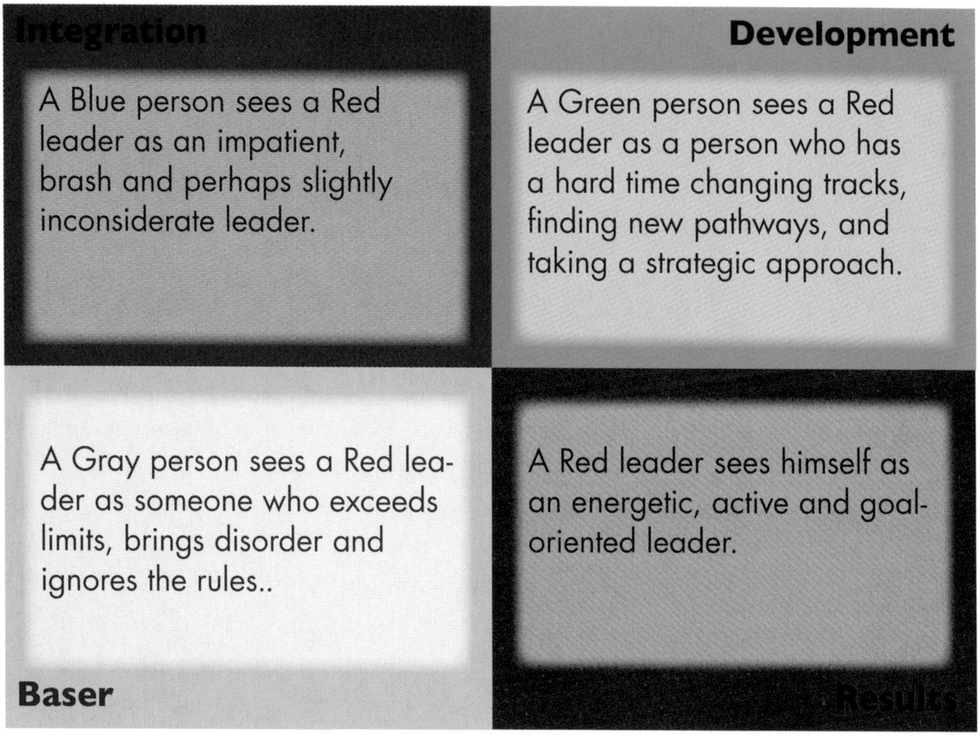

| Integration | Development |
|---|---|
| A Blue person sees a Red leader as an impatient, brash and perhaps slightly inconsiderate leader. | A Green person sees a Red leader as a person who has a hard time changing tracks, finding new pathways, and taking a strategic approach. |
| A Gray person sees a Red leader as someone who exceeds limits, brings disorder and ignores the rules.. | A Red leader sees himself as an energetic, active and goal-oriented leader. |
| **Baser** | **Results** |

Then I described in the Gray and Green areas above how a Red leader can expect to be perceived by people whose main focus is in these two other areas.

The idea behind the following exercise is to illustrate and make you aware of the fact that the active, goal-oriented behavior valued by a Red leader can have consequences which are seen from the viewpoint of other people and not from the viewpoint of the Red leader. A Blue person (subordinate, colleague, superior) sees the same behavior, but perceives it and acts according to the feelings the behavior engenders in him/her. If you look at the key words in the Blue area of the Focus Model – fellowship, harmony, trust, understanding, helpful, etc. – and then attempt to look at a Red leader through Blue eyeglasses, it is easy to understand that this person will be perceived as energetic and goal-oriented, yes, but also as brash and maybe just a little inconsiderate.

So it can be quite productive to learn to see yourself through the eyes of other people. You have to learn to see yourself through three different pairs of glasses: the three pairs you aren't already wearing. If your highest score is in the Red field, then you should learn to see yourself through Gray, Blue and Green glasses. If your highest score is in the Gray field, then you should learn to see yourself through Red, Blue and Green glasses, and so on. This next exercise gives you a method to use.

 *Exercise 9*

### Figure 40. How you see yourself (Draw your Leadership Profile)

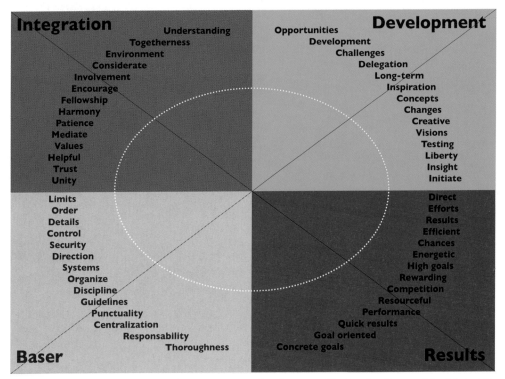

The first step is to draw your Leadership profile in the Focus Model in Figure 40. Now take the key words in the field in which you had the highest score and write a short description of the good things you see in yourself, like in the Red leader example in Figure 39. Write down your perception of yourself in the relevant box in the model in Figure 41.

The Leader's Mental Scorecard. © Finn Havaleschka.

## Figure 41. How you see yourself

(Write down how you perceive yourself in the relevant box)

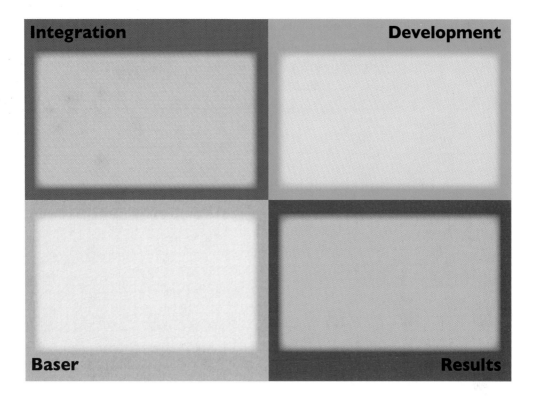

After you describe how you see yourself in one or perhaps two (if your profile is equally strong in two areas) of the empty boxes in Figure 41, then try to look at yourself through each of the three other pairs of eyeglasses, so to speak. Use the key words in the model as your starting point, and try to imagine how your behavior would be perceived by a person in the field diagonally opposite to yours, and then by people in the other two areas. Record your thoughts in the appropriate boxes in Figure 42.

## Figure 42. How other people see you
(Describe yourself seen through four different pairs of glasses)

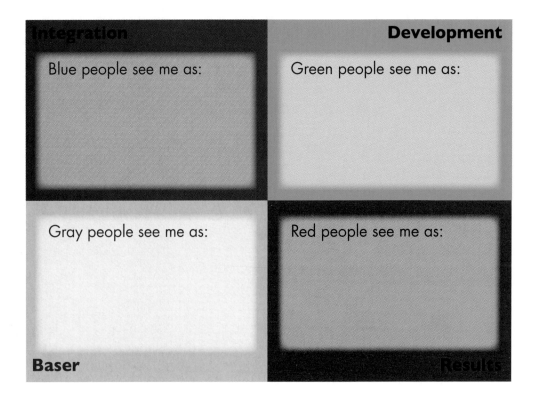

I really hope that you will work painstakingly and seriously with this exercise. Experience shows that it is a very effective way to learn to see yourself through the eyes of other people and understand why you aren't always perceived in the way you think or judged on the basis of the same values you judge yourself by.

In any case, this insight is something you must have before you can learn to find your leadership sweet spot – to the point where you can figuratively move out into the focus area and practice the type of leadership that is most appropriate for the situation and the people involved in it.

## Happiness as Motivation

Another way to obtain the necessary insight into yourself could be to look at what drives you: what motivates you to do the things you do. Many, many books have been written about motivation. We'll skip them here. The only thing we can say for sure is that no matter who you are, where in the world you come from, how rich or poor you are, what your social or political convictions are, or what position you hold, you have one thing in common with everyone else on this earth: you seek happiness. I once spent a great deal of time looking at this side of leadership and life, and my conclusion was as follows:

> Motivation comes from the pleasure we anticipate,
> in the expectation that something will succeed
> – and make us happier.

It is Kierkegaard revisited. Joyful anticipation! On the other hand, the opposite is also true, but this is something I have only recently accepted. Our behavior may be determined to a greater degree by our endeavor to hold onto what we have. In that case, we can turn the above statement around:

> Motivation comes from the unpleasant feeling we get
> when we expect something to be taken from us – and that
> makes us unhappy.

Thus one could say that what motivates our behavior has two sources: pleasure and unpleasantness. People differ in the way they seek out what is pleasant and seek to avoid what is unpleasant, but – again – there are certain common features. We can simplify things by looking at the four areas of the Focus Model. Baser people look for happiness and try to keep unpleasantness at bay by being in control. They plan for the future in order to avoid surprises. They go into all the details and follow the rules, and when they go shopping, there is always enough left over to pay the rent. They may live with a job they aren't ecstatic about, but they keep it and will fight to keep it the way it is because they do not dare to jump into something they feel unsure of. Or, if we take an example from the personal sphere, they live in a relationship which causes them to suffer more unpleasantness than pleasure, but they stay in the relationship anyway. No matter what, it is vital to maintain that feeling of being in control and a certain degree of predictability: at least you know what you can expect.

The behavior of Results individuals follows the same mechanisms. Their behavior has a single motivation: to optimize happiness and avoid unhappiness. Results achievers seek happiness by being the best one in the group they compare themselves with. Happiness is being number one, getting things done, obtaining results, making use of themselves, being energetic and goal-oriented, and seeking praise in order to avoid criticism. That is how Results people keep unhappiness at bay. They fight to maintain their position: anything else is connected with unpleasantness.

Integrators seek happiness and seek to keep unhappiness at bay through social relations. As long as people don't quarrel, but can talk about things, sympathize with each other's thoughts and feelings, understand each other, are considerate and show solicitude, then they will surely be happy – someday. They feel that they can at least keep the unpleasantness down to a tolerable level if they avoid conflict and do their best to live up to other people's expectations.

Development people are certain that happiness can be found in insight and in the opportunities to mold the future. They believe that once you understand how things really are, and you then formulate your visions for the future on that basis, then you are the master of your own destiny. Happiness is being able to see and help chart the general course. To avoid unpleasantness, one has to plunge into one's own world of ideas so deep that one completely loses contact with the reality.[43]

---

[43] Unlike the development paradigm of the 1970s and 1980s, which was especially characterized by a belief that people's main motivation was and is that if we just develop our flexibility, our willingness to change, our ability and willingness to become involved, and our ability to say yes and no to things and to take responsibility, then we will also become more harmonious, develop a higher degree of autonomy, etc. (see the quote on page 14). However, although practice doesn't count for much in the world of science until you can assign numbers to it, I have come to believe that the main drive behind motivation for a very many people is much more based on limiting unpleasantness than expanding happiness, which doesn't quite fit in with the development paradigm claim that we are developing ourselves towards "a less self-centered perception and interaction with other people." As a result, obviously, many people are better motivated by the fear of losing something and thus by threats than by promises or prospects of more happiness.

And since we are all striving for happiness but have different ways and means of obtaining it, then situations easily occur where we each stand in our own corner calling to the others in their corners. The Results achiever stands in his Red corner, shouting, "Hey, guys, c'mon over here! We got it going on! We live in the fast lane, in the present! We get results and we don't worry so much about the future! Live life while you can – that' the way to find happiness!"

The Baser in his corner answers, "Uh, no…it seems as bit chaotic. Come over here! Things are safe and secure here; we always have enough to pay the rent; we don't get in over our heads; we keep the wolf away from the door!"

At that point, the Integrator insistently explains from his Blue corner: "No, hey, guys, come up here! It's cozy; we have a nice time here; we care about each other; we talk about things. Everyone's equal and of equal value. We don't exclude anyone; we stick together; we comfort each other when things go wrong. Together we find happiness!"

While these different views are flying around the three corners, the Developer interrupts with: "Where are you at, guys? What are you basing all that on? No, come up here! You'll get insight and an overview. We help and inspire each other here to see how things are connected at a general level – this is where we make the future! This is the way to happiness!"

Thus you could say we are all seeking happiness from our own points of view. Our tool is our personality, with all the opportunities and limitations that involves. With that in mind, think about this for a minute:

How many times have you said no to happiness because it came from the wrong corner?

# VIII. Where Are Your Subordinates
## The needs and personality of those under your leadership

As mentioned above a whole truckload of times, one prerequisite for good leadership is that we are able to go to the place where our subordinates are and meet them there. As an introduction to this section's exercises, I would like to give you an idea of some of my own personal experiences. I must admit that the following descriptions are fairly black and white. The idea, however, is not to provide a detailed and in-depth description of the behavior of each type of leader and their way to lead other people, but simply to get you to start thinking some thoughts about yourself, your leadership style and its suitability for use with different types of subordinates.

## Results Leaders

Picture the Focus Model now, with the Results leader in his red field in the lower right corner. He's an energetic guy, full of enthusiasm and drive. Testosterone is rushing through his veins; something's got to give; he has to make things happen, has to get results, has to be faster, better and stronger than all the others. Results leaders also want to have fun, and the only way to do that is to compete while we're busy pulling each other's legs. It is friendly teasing, and we play for the right to make fun of the loser.

The picture I'm drawing might be a bit too exaggerated for these characters to seem like real people. All right, but there are also Results leaders that take things more seriously. They are a stubborn, persistent and highly goal-oriented type. Once the goal is defined and the course has been laid, then there are no excuses. What they have promised to do, we do. They discipline ourselves and don't flinch when it hurts. Yielding, lowering their ambitions and accepting new, revised goals, admitting to the outside world that they can't do what they promised – it is a major setback. "One should be able to take people at their word!" They play for glory.

What happens if these Results leaders find out they are losing and won't win the right to make fun of the loser? Let me show you the profile of such a Results leader: see Figure 43.

The Leader's Mental Scorecard. © Finn Havaleschka.

## Figure 43. Profile of a Results leader

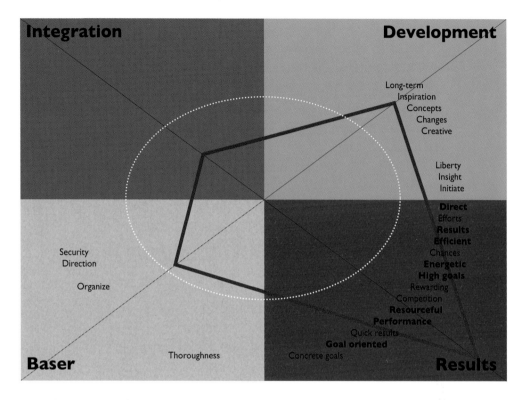

It is the same profile and same person as I showed you in the first part of the book. The profile shows the person's normal focus, which is primarily red and a little green. He deselected all statements about Baser leadership (except for three) and all 16 statements about Integrator leadership. In other words, these types of leadership are quite foreign to his nature. Integration and Baser leadership are something he rejects quite consciously. If this is true, then what happens when he comes under fire, i.e. if his usual focus, the one dictated by his personality, doesn't produce the desired results? Would he drop the Red style of leadership and consider the alternatives? No way! He has rejected these alternatives and never really practiced them. He is like a soccer player that has never practiced kicking the ball with his left foot. He doesn't feel comfortable doing that, so he will do everything he can to put himself in a position where he can kick with his right. The same goes for this manager: if he feels pressured, we will see him redouble his efforts to reach his goal. So that he can kick with his right foot, he will invest more resources and demand that his subordinates run faster, work more, take chances, cut a few corners, bend some rules and promise some discounts. The chance that he will reach his goal and the satisfaction he expects to feel when he does so are strong motivational factors for Results leaders. Naturally, they don't want to lose the right to tease the loser, either. So they grit their teeth and pump a little more adrenaline into their blood. They don't stop and ask how their subordinates are doing. They apply their own standards: "If they can't take the pace, that's too bad; they can pack their bags if they want."

Results leaders that reject Integrator leadership don't think so much about whether their subordinates understand why it is so important to reach the targets that have been set. They simply take it for granted that everyone knows their what the goals are. (Otherwise they would ask, right?) They also take it for granted that everyone believes it is important to achieve the objectives that have been set – and preferably a little more than the objectives. The first thing they think of is not whether some of his subordinates have obligations other than their jobs, e.g. whether they have to pick up their kids at daycare or have a family life based on other principles and values than their own. And funnily enough, for many Results leaders, holidays and vacations come at an extremely inconvenient time, year after year. Believe me: I speak from personal experience.

Because he has the personality he does, and because he hasn't practiced kicking with his left foot, then a Red leader will move even further out into the Red corner, especially when he feels under pressure. There he stands, shouting to the others: "Come over here! We need to move; we need to keep moving; this is urgent; we won't reach our goal! Hurry up; put more effort into it; get somebody else to pick up your kids at nursery school!" It hasn't even occurred to him that he could go to where his Integrator subordinate or his Baser subordinate are standing. He figures they should damn well be able to see what's going on.

Before you can learn to move your focus, you must first become aware of the things you are *not* focusing on. Then you can begin to practice kicking the ball with your left foot. Practice won't make you a left-footed soccer player: it won't change your personality, but it can help you handle high-pressure situations by looking at the situation and then learning to meet your coworkers – not halfway, but where *they* are, and thus fully utilize their knowledge, resources and competencies.

The profile drawn in black in Figure 44 illustrates that this Red leader needs to let go of some of his Results energy so that he can instead use it to apply the other types of leadership.

## Figure 44. The focus alternatives for Red leaders (The black profile)

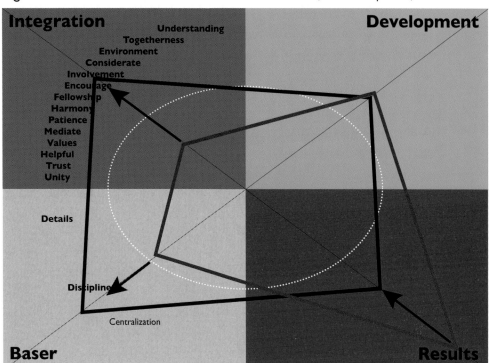

Of course, it is not just Results leaders that have difficulty moving into corners that are not their own. This applies to the other types of leaders as well. As mentioned previously, a manager seldom focuses on one area alone. Usually, people focus on a combination of two areas, and a small percentage of people focus on three. The above description of a Results leader is based on reality, but his normal daily behavior is, naturally, a great deal more complex than described here. I am exaggerating certain things on purpose in order to emphasize the consequences of a lack of focus on the other leadership styles.

## Baser Leaders

Quite naturally, Baser leaders also want to see results, but the playing field is completely different here. They do not deviate from their plans, and they would rather budget too low than too high. They seldom compromise; they write and stick to the rules; they demand discipline; and they control and verify down to the smallest detail. If things go as planned, then that's good, and the reason it went well – they say – was the accuracy and thoroughness they insisted on. What happens, though, when things don't go so well? What does this type of leader focus on then? Will he move up into the Green corner and give his subordinates more freedom and more opportunities to make independent decisions, use their creativity, be innovative, and to change the basic parameters and rules for how to solve tasks? Hardly! That approach to life, leadership and the solution of problems and crises are not his style, even though precisely that kind of leadership might help his people resolve a situation. In a crisis, strong Baser leaders often try to tackle the problems by administering the same kind of medicine that helped create the crisis in the first place. They just pile on bigger doses of it: more control, more verification, more guidelines and more centralization.

If from this description you recognize a tendency in yourself toward practicing mainly Baser leadership, then look at the key words and phrases in the other three areas and think about whether maybe you should practice kicking with your left foot – or pitching with your left hand, if you are more into baseball.

## Integrator Leaders

Integrator leaders also want to see results, but it has to happen in cooperation with others. It is important to agree on the playing field, to ensure understanding and acceptance of the objectives, to involve and motivate people, to be considerate, to be patient and to show understanding. At meetings, everyone at the table discusses problems – Integrator leaders don't issue orders. They trust people and accept their social differences. They are tolerant, have an open-door policy and don't make what they consider unreasonable demands. What happens if this leadership style does not suit the reality or the workers, and the results don't happen? Would this leader go down into the Red corner and suddenly start making demands, getting down to business, set performance standards and show consistency? Hardly! Or would he move down into the Gray corner and start controlling and verifying, beat his fear of conflict, demand discipline, lay down rules, demand accuracy and precision, and trim excesses? Probably not. It is more likely that even more meetings would be held at which people would talk a lot about what is causing the problems. They would come up with many possible solutions, but would these solutions be implemented with the necessary firmness?

If you are an Integrator leader and recognize some of this behavior from your own leadership style, then you should look at the key words in the other three areas in the Focus Model. Use the descriptions and the following exercises to learn a bit about the other types of leadership.

## Development Leaders

Development leaders also want results, but they want to go the creative route to get them. To them, it is important to see the opportunities, not the limitations. Their attitude is if you can just put the right concepts together and if you are innovative; think long-term; have visions; get rid of or refurbish some of the old methods and introduce new, more flexible rules; and give your subordinates challenges to tackle and freedom, then you will see results. But how does a Development leader react if they *don't* see results? Does he move down into the Red corner, put on his steel-toed boots, roll up his leaves and take the lead in handling the practical things that bring home the bacon? Or does he move down into the Gray corner to check that all the details are in order and ensure that his subordinates have well-defined areas of responsibilities that they are familiar with and feel confident about handling? Does he make sure that the logistics work, that activities are properly coordinated, and that the company really has the resources necessary to implement its visions? Does he go into the Gray area to find out whether it could have been the lack of any of these things that resulted in the company overspending and therefore now unable to deliver the promised results?

Can you picture this? With a Development leader, you're on your way into cyberspace. The rocket has blasted off, some of the passengers are tense and most are confused; there is chaos behind us and we only have enough fuel to get halfway there. Still, it's fun and it's challenging, especially for the people with the same temperament as the Development leader. If you are a Development leader, then make sure this kind of thing doesn't happen to you and your people – *too* often.

Again, these **are** exaggerated and simplified descriptions, but think of their purpose while you're reading them: to make you see the strong and weak sides of the different focus areas, especially your own, of course. Nothing is bad or good in all this. It is only inappropriate or inexpedient when your focus doesn't fit the situation, when you don't adapt your approach to suit your subordinates' needs, and you can't adapt your approach to the problem and situation at hand. In the following exercise, I want you to use the model to identify the needs and personalities of the people who work under you, and accordingly to make you aware of the advantages and disadvantages of your leadership style.

 *Exercise 10*

## Where are your subordinates?

Start by taking a number of copies of the Focus Model at the back of the book (Document 12 or 13), one for each of your subordinates. Then find a place where you can sit by yourself and focus: turn all your attention on thinking about one person at a time. Underline the key words or phrases in the model that you think best describe the person's behavior, attitudes, preferences and values. To ensure that you stick to what is most important, try to limit the number of key words or phrases you underline to six per person. Then find four to six key words or phrases that in your opinion best describe what the person is not. When you are done, you are ready to start thinking about where you can go in the Focus Model to meet this person. See the example in Figure 45. Words and concepts marked with + are words and concepts which this leader believes describe the subordinate's behavior and motivates him. Words marked with - indicates what the subordinate is not and what supposedly will de-motivates him.

Figure 45. Subordinate NN, sales assistant (Example)

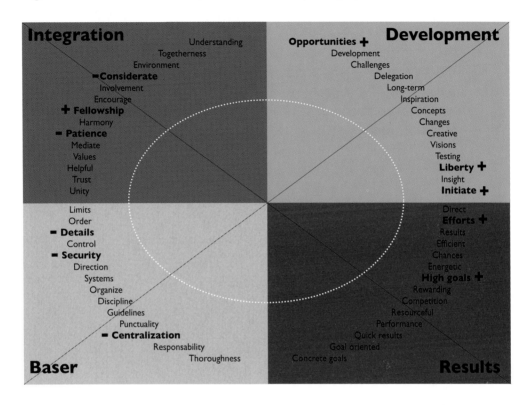

This example shows a manager who describes a subordinate's behavior and motives by the following concepts:

| | |
|---|---|
| **+ Fellowship** | **+ Opportunities** |
| **+ Liberty** | **+ High goals** |
| **+ Initiate** | **+ Efforts** |

And describes what the subordinate is **not** by the concepts:

| | |
|---|---|
| **▬ Patience** | **▬ Security** |
| **▬ Considerate** | **▬ Centralization** |
| **▬ Details** | |

The concepts illustrate what motivates this subordinate and thus indirectly show what he is good at and what he probably is not so good at. The question is whether his manager gives him the opportunity to fully exploit these characteristics. The next thing, naturally, is to consider whether this person's underlined qualities are well suited to the job and tasks he is supposed to perform. Luckily, this employee doesn't work in the accounting department, but has quite a lively job in sales. Once you have taken one sheet per worker and underlined the relevant words and phrases for each one, then go through them again, this time to consider what type of leadership would support and motivate each person best. Jot your thoughts down in Document 14 at the back of this book. See the example in Diagram 14 below which shows how I did this for the person evaluated in Figure 45.

## Diagram 14. Motivating and demotivating leadership of Green subordinate (Example)

| Characteristics of subordinate: | Characteristics of subordinate: |
|---|---|
| **+ Fellowship**<br>**− Patient**<br>**− Considerate**<br><br>*Therefore: Involve him in discussions and the work, let him come forward with his ideas... Accept impatience and try to make him moderate his bluntness. Talk to him about that.* | **+ Opportunities**<br>**+ Liberty**<br>**+ Initiate** |
| Characteristics of subordinate: | Characteristics of subordinate: |
| **− Details**<br>**− Security**<br>**− Centralization**<br><br>*Therefore: Don't give him too many rules to follow, tasks that force him to dwell on details, limits that are too restrictive, or anything that limits his ability to work independently...* | **+ High goals**<br>**+ Efforts**<br><br>*Therefore: Make ambitious demands on him, give him high goals to reach...* |

The words that describe the person in Diagram 16 come from the Development area of the Focus Model. The key words and phrases and where they are in the Focus Model can help you figure out what will motivate or de-motivate each subordinate.

So now the idea is to work your way systematically and with concentration through each one of your subordinates in this manner. Take a photocopy of the Focus Model (Document 13) for each subordinate and underline the key words you believe best describe that person. Now look at Document 14 at the back of the book, which looks like Diagram 14. If most of the concepts that you underline for a certain person are in the Gray area of the Focus Model, than take a copy of the part of Document 14 that shows the Gray corner of the Focus Model and write in the empty boxes what you think will motivate and demotivate this person. It takes a bit of time to do, but I guarantee you that it is time well spent.

## Interviews

It is important that you did the "paperwork" described above for a subordinate before you interview him or her. Just as you previously discussed the Mirror Profiles your subordinates did for you or of you, now you should give each person the opportunity to talk about what motivates or demotivates him/her. Ask this person to underline the six key words or phrases that he/she believes best describes what motivates him/her and the six key words or phrases that best describe what demotivates him/her.

Take some copies of the Focus Model and sit down with one subordinate at a time. Tell the person briefly about the Model and explain what the purpose of this interview is. Give the person time to make his/her choices and underline them without your intervening or asking questions. It would be a good idea to leave the room and let him/her do it alone. Afterwards, ask the person to explain his/her choices. During this part of the process, it is vital that you are listening carefully. You can have your own opinions and attitudes, **but you must keep them to yourself**. The rule is that you may only ask "(w)h" questions, i.e. questions that start with those letters:

- Why
- How?
- Where
- When?

Ask for explanations, examples and clarifications. Listen, take notes and ask.

After the interview, compare your observations from Exercise 9 with the key words the person him/herself underlined. When you have done that, you will have a fairly good idea about where this person is in the Focus Model, and you will be well prepared to take the next step: practicing your ability to go to the place where this person is and meet him/her there.

The Leader's Mental Scorecard. © Finn Havaleschka.

And remember:

> No one, not even your children, is born into this world
> to satisfy your expectations.

Therefore, if your subordinates don't act, behave, make choices, prioritize the way you expect them to do – you better re-evaluate your expectations.

# Part Three
## Where Do You Want to Go

# What the four types are thinking and saying

No matter where in the world we are from, what different languages we speak or differences in upbringing, values and attitudes, we all have one thing in common. We all strive for happiness and joy - just as we all strive to avoid pain and unhappiness.

Another thing we have in common is that we spend more time and energy avoiding unhappiness and pain, and try to hold on to what we already have instead of searching for happiness. Only few of us let go of what we possess, without having a guarantee that we will get more in return.

A third thing we have in common is the fact that our approach to happiness and our efforts to avoid pain are determined mostly by our personality and not by our upbringing. Our approach doesn't seem to change. It is constant and predictable.  So in most situations Einstein's definition of insanity applies: To use the same behavior and expect different results.

However, what makes us happy and what makes us feel pain, and how we pursue happiness as well as attempt to avoid pain differs from person to person. In the following you can see and read about the four types of personalities and their approach to happiness – avoiding pain.

# What the Baser Personality thinks and says!

The Leader's Mental Scorecard. © Finn Havaleschka.

The Leader's Mental Scorecard. © Finn Havaleschka.

The Leader's Mental Scorecard. © Finn Havaleschka.

The Leader's Mental Scorecard. © Finn Havaleschka.

# What the Result Personality thinks and says!

The Leader's Mental Scorecard. © Finn Havaleschka.

The Leader's Mental Scorecard. © Finn Havaleschka.

The Leader's Mental Scorecard. © Finn Havaleschka.

# What the Integrator Personality thinks and says!

The Leader's Mental Scorecard. © Finn Havaleschka.

© Garuda Research Institute - info@garudahr.com

The Leader's Mental Scorecard. © Finn Havaleschka.

The Leader's Mental Scorecard. © Finn Havaleschka.

# What the Developer Personality thinks and says!

The Leader's Mental Scorecard. © Finn Havaleschka.

The Leader's Mental Scorecard. © Finn Havaleschka.

The Leader's Mental Scorecard. © Finn Havaleschka.

# IX. What Does the Situation Require
## Focus, job requirements and situational needs

You have probably already thought about whether the job you have is ideal for you in view of your natural focus and your personality. People with a Baser focus are better at handling work that requires systematic, detail-oriented and structured work. People with a Results focus are best at work that requires pragmatic action, work where things are to be moved and done right now, and work whose results can and have to be seen and achieved almost from one hour to the next. People with an Integrator focus are best at tasks that require cooperation, listening, a coordination of ideas and interests, and solicitude toward others. People with a Development focus do best in jobs that require innovative thinking and changes to be made.

This is, of course, a simplified description of things that are a lot more complex in reality. Nevertheless, the Focus Model can help you zero in on just how much the job you have suits your personality and temperament. When there is a good fit between job and person, success is easy, but the poorer the fit, the more difficult it is. That's when you run into obstacles, crises and resistance, and that's when other people criticize you and block your moves. So, really, you probably already know how well your job suits your personality. Still, the Focus Model can help make you more aware of and knowledgeable about why things are the way they are. Why do you feel good about and do well at your job - or don't do as well as you would like to? Where is it you have to yield, to go against the grain of your personality in a compromise, why and for how long, if you want to be successful?

After having tested and interviewed thousands of people and analyzed the relationship between their personality on the one side and their job and job success on the other, as early as the late 1980s I could clearly see that it would be a lot easier to fit the job to the personality than change the personality to suit the job. Basically, it is easier to take the work within an area of responsibility and divide it into tasks that can then go to different people based on their personality, preferred focus and skills than it is to adapt (develop) their personalities and focus to the different tasks. The faster the authorities on psychology and leadership theory reach this same conclusion, the faster we will see new knowledge being developed and applied to leadership and organizational theory and practice.

In very many jobs, it is still the old and well-established professional boundaries and traditional organizational and leadership-theory thinking that determine the duties and responsibilities that make up the job that goes with the name of the position and thus – by definition – what duties and responsibilities the person holding the position has. However, if the duties and responsibilities that go with a position more or less require a talent for all four types of focus, then it is obvious that no single person would be able to perform all those duties and responsibilities successfully.

So, forget the name of the position (which is often what defines salary, status, profession and title), and take a number of naturally cohesive tasks, tasks that have a natural connection with each other, and bring them together under a single area of responsibility. Then allow the workers dealing with that area of responsibility request the individual tasks that interest them and which they think suit their abilities, level of ambition, etc.[44]

---

[44] Garuda Research Institute has developed a group discussion tool that makes exactly this process possible. We call this tool the GROUP Profile, and it lays the framework for and then initiates a structured process whereby each worker, considering his or her own skills and ambitions, can offer to take on the tasks that interest him or her most, and then group of participants divide up and coordinate the tasks in the way that is optimal based on the total spectrum of competencies available in the group.

## What kind of focus does your job require?

In the following exercise, you and your coach are to analyze your job and list the requirements you find that your job has with respect to focus: what kind(s) of focus does your job require you to have? First, picture yourself rising up above the Focus Model and then landing again right in the middle of it. Then think about the degree to which your work, your responsibilities and your duties require the first, second, third and/or fourth types of focus in the model, and you will probably realize that you need to focus on - pay more attention to - one or two of the areas more than the others.

Now, the systematic way to do this is as follows. Each focus area can be given a number of points, from minus 24 to plus 24. Your task now is to allot points to the four focus areas in a way that reflects the focus that you think, feel or observe that your job requires. Start by giving points to the focus area that you (and your coach) think is the most important one. Then assign points to the other three areas. To help you, below is a brief description of each of the focus areas. First is the Baser area.

### Baser Focus

The parts of your job that require Baser focus are those in which you must spend time on and be aware of tasks that need structuring, planning, systematizing, making and following schedules, tasks which require you and your coworkers to know about and observe certain rules or limitations, and tasks which generally require people to weigh, measure, calculate and check things. It could, for example, be physical objects, numbers, words or other information that needs to be processed, stored, moved and always be at the right place at certain times and in the correct amounts. Thus Baser leadership requires a focus on security and accuracy right down to the smallest detail. Other key words are precision, order, control, systems, organization, planning, knowing and following rules, instructions, and remaining within given frameworks and structures. Based on this description, how necessary would you say it is to focus on Baser leadership in your job?

| -24 | | 18 | | 12 | | 6 | | 0 | | 6 | | 12 | | 18 | | +24 |
|---|---|---|---|---|---|---|---|---|---|---|---|---|---|---|---|---|

Less important                                              Extremely important

The Leader's Mental Scorecard. © Finn Havaleschka.

## Results Focus

The parts of your job that require Results focus are the parts where you need to spend time on work that has to be done right now and where you constantly have to ensure that short-term objectives are being achieved. These are tasks where it is vital for things to be delivered on time; where products have to be done on time; where ideas, products and concepts have to be sold right here and right now; and where you, though your leadership as you practice it, must ensure and monitor that you and your subordinates always utilize existing resources optimally and obtain the best possible output.

Results tasks involve taking specific steps to reach clearly defined goals within a specified short-term deadline by utilizing certain resources. Results work entails the necessity to be efficient and effective and to produce results in the short term.

Based on this description, how necessary would you say it is to focus on Results leadership in your job?

| -24 | | 18 | | 12 | | 6 | | 0 | | 6 | | 12 | | 18 | | +24 |
|---|---|---|---|---|---|---|---|---|---|---|---|---|---|---|---|---|

Less important                                                        Extremely important

## ■ Integrator Focus

The parts of your job that require Integrator focus are where it is your responsibility that everyone generally works well together and where it is your job to create team spirit, avoid or solve conflicts; to get people to help each other across boundaries of status, function and fields of responsibility; to take different social and psychological factors into consideration; to be aware of other people's feelings and motives; to be solicitous of people; to ensure that other people get the attention they feel they deserve; to negotiate between involved parties with different interests, attitudes, values; and so on.

Integrator tasks require leadership with a focus on understanding, patience, listening, being sympathetic, and the ability to hold back on expressing your own point of view. The key words for your job responsibilities are ensuring a sense of community, integration, mediation, togetherness, communicating, and gaining understanding for objectives, concepts, strategies, methods and means.

Based on the description above, how necessary would you say it is to focus on Integrator leadership in your job?

| -24 | | 18 | | 12 | | 6 | | 0 | | 6 | | 12 | | 18 | | +24 |
|---|---|---|---|---|---|---|---|---|---|---|---|---|---|---|---|---|

Less important                                                                 Extremely important ■

## Development Focus

The parts of your job that require Development focus are where you work with strategy problems and with things that are visionary, general and take the organization forward, and where you and your subordinates are supposed to analyze, come up with proposals and be in charge of making changes, coming up with new methods and creating new concepts. This work involves analyzing existing structures, limits and administrative routines with a view to introducing change, with you in charge of implementing these changes.

Development tasks require acts of leadership and decisions that create an overview that promotes creativity and visionary thinking in subordinates, and it requires time spent focusing on the communication of messages and promoting enthusiasm in subordinates.

Based on this description, how necessary would you say it is to focus on Development leadership in your job?

| -24 | | 18 | | 12 | | 6 | | 0 | | 6 | | 12 | | 18 | | +24 |
|---|---|---|---|---|---|---|---|---|---|---|---|---|---|---|---|---|

Less important                                          Extremely important

Now you take each score from the four scales above and transfer them to the Focus Model in Figure 46 that relates to the focus area in question. If you gave the Development area 12 points on the Green scale just above, then put a dot at 12 on the axis that cuts through the Green Development area in the upper right-hand corner of the figure.

Now connect the four dots to make a profile in the model and discuss your findings with your coach. Of course, it is vital that you concentrate on the area or areas where the profile shows that there is a gap between your natural focus – the focus you have because of the personality you have - and the leadership focus your job entails. The question is whether you, when the situation calls for it, are able to move from your natural focus and over into the focus area or areas that your analysis shows that you should be able to cover as well. Perhaps this is something that you already do.

To make yourself aware of the general advantages and disadvantages in

## Figure 46. The leadership requirements of your job
(Job Requirement Profile)

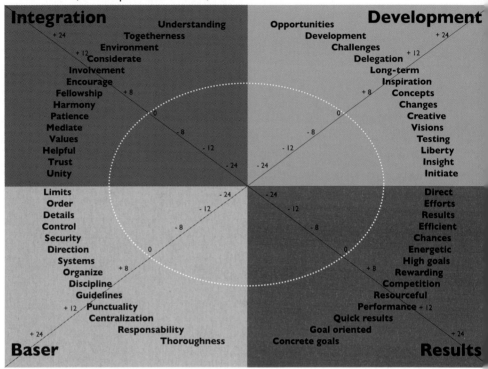

the differences between your Leadership Profile and your Job Requirements Profile, go back to the results of your work with the Exercise "**What you dislike about other types**" on page 154. Reviewing this exercise will also give you a good feel for what the strong and weak sides of your current leadership focus are compared with the requirements you are analyzing. When you put together your Mental Scorecard, of course, you should be aware of these things

## The Two Things the Situation Requires

The reason for drawing your Job Requirement Profile is to what kind(s) of focus your job generally requires. In addition to this, certain requirements may arise in certain situations, requirements that especially become apparent if things aren't going the way they should. In Part One above (Figure 10 on page 85), I explained a situation in which you could use the Model to determine the needs of a subordinate – where and how a leader could go, figuratively, to the place where his subordinate is, where the subordinate's focus is – and then to determine what is needed in the situation at hand, i.e. the actual circumstances of the situation. In this situation, people were waiting for one of their coworkers to finish developing a new part for a product. Everyone who needed this new part was pretty much in a holding pattern. The guy they were all waiting for felt highly pressured and uncertain in his job and the possible consequences to his job and his future, which – of course – hardly improved his work efficiency. I have written a description of the situation in the model in Figure 47.

## Figure 47. The Leadership Model

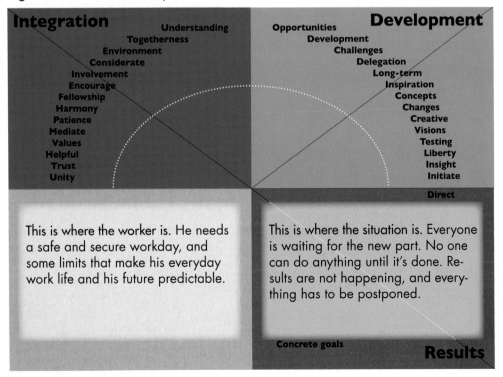

The Leader's Mental Scorecard. © Finn Havaleschka.

What I would like to illustrate with this example is that all leadership situations consist of two components, or two requirements that must be fulfilled. One is the need the worker has, and the other is what you want to achieve in the given situation – what is required of you. In the example above, the worker's needs are described in the Gray area and the requirements of the situation in the Red area. The objective in our example situation is to finish the new part as quickly as possible while also mitigating the negative consequences, both the practical and the human ones (the people who aren't getting the part on time are furious because we're wasting their time, too).

Unfortunately, what often happens is that the leader feels, focuses on and acts upon the demands of the situation only; he tries to solve the problem from the place where he is in the model, and he tries to solve the problem from there using his/her normal focus. What this can easily – and subconsciously – result in is an attitude that everyone else has got it all wrong. In other words, for example, the worker didn't understand how important it all was and should have put more time and energy into it, and the client (the customer, the one waiting) is inflexible, not at all understanding how such a thing could happen and making completely unreasonable demands.

 *Exercise 13*

## Identifying the two things the situation requires

Situations change all the time, which means that the kind of focus needed does, too. As a result, it can be difficult to be prepared in every situation. You must be ready to tackle situations as they arise, asking yourself: What kind of focus does the worker in question have? What kind of focus does the situation demand? Look at the example in Diagram 17. Put yourself in the area that represents your permanent position, your preferred focus. When you then run into a situation that you have some doubt as to how you should tackle, then stop, take a copy of Document 15 at the back of the book, and think about the two types of requirements here: what the situation requires and what the worker in question requires. Then write down these requirements in the relevant boxes. This is a way to help you determine the best possible method for you to go about tackling the situation.

## Diagram 17. Identifying the needs of the worker and the situation
(What type of need should be fulfilled in the situation you are in right now?) Example

| Integration Requirements the situation): | Your own focus: |
|---|---|
| We need to create solidarity and understanding about teamwork and what our goals are. | |
| **Baser Requirements (the situation):**<br><br>We have received rules from HQ that need to be implemented and followed up on. | **Results Requirements (the subordinate):**<br><br>Wants to see results, wants to earn money, wants praise, wants to be #1, hates losing. |

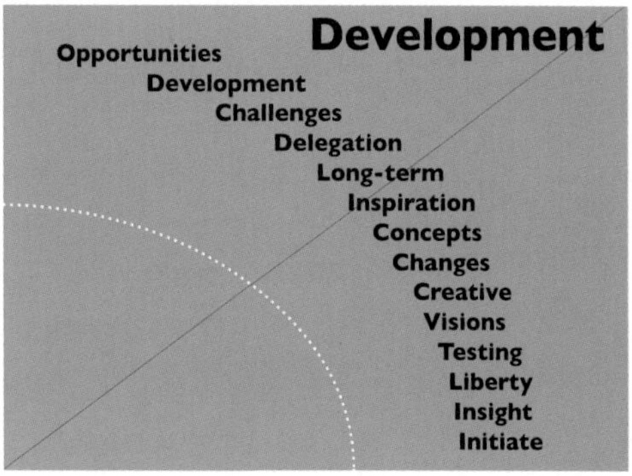

In the example, Diagram 17, I put the key words for a Green leader in the model's Development field. Put the key words and phrases for your own focus in the area in the model in which your natural focus lies. The example illustrates a situation in which new rules come down from headquarters that are to be followed in connection with sales and making offers. All orders and offers are processed by a group of workers, one of whom is having difficulty accepting and following the new rules.

Now work together with your coach and try to find a situation from your everyday work life that you have been in, lived through, and thus know the consequences of. Then ask yourself the following questions:

- Where was your own focus?
- What were the needs and focus of the subordinate(s) in question?
- What are the requirements of the situation?
- How could you have done it better?

The diagram filled in above can be found blank at the back of the book (Document 15). Any time you find yourself in a leadership situation in which you are a little unsure, then take a copy of the blank diagram and spend a couple of minutes analyzing the situation. This will teach you to see and solve leadership problems from several different angles.

# X. The Leader's Mental Scorecard

How to go to the places your subordinates are

In Part One, I explained the practical and theoretical principles behind the Mental Scorecard. It's all about learning to move away from your usual area of focus and to another area (where depends on the situation) – moving away from where you feel at home and to a place where it is more difficult to become acclimatized. It's about learning to adapt yourself, to dress appropriately for the situation, and to adjust to other habits, values and ways of doing things. It is best to learn the lingo – kick with your left leg – by speaking it, to learn by doing. We must throw ourselves into the pool, so to speak: not without thinking, not unsystematically and not unprepared, but still immerse ourselves. The learning I want you to do now cannot be done in a classroom or a social vacuum; it has to be done in practice, in an interaction with others. One step at a time. We listen, we learn a few words, we pronounce them, we put them together to make sentences, and finally we put the sentences together to make explanations. These are – figuratively – the principles behind the Mental Scorecard.

The Mental Scorecard consists of well-defined leadership actions that are carried out in practice after a systematic mental and practical process of preparation. The leadership actions are defined relative to the four focus areas of the Focus Model. If, for example, you are decidedly a Green leader, then you must begin by 1) making yourself aware of, 2) preparing to carry out, and 3) carrying out Blue, Gray and/or Red leadership actions. If your lowest score is in the Blue area, for example, then this is where you would start your work. There is an example of a Mental Scorecard at the end of Part One. The two Blue leadership actions in Diagram 18 below are taken from this particular scorecard.

## Diagram 18. Example Blue leadership actions

| Sit· | Color | Focus, Calendar Weeks 17 and 18, 2004 | Points | |
|---|---|---|---|---|
| | | | + | - |
| 6 | | **Action:** Involving coworkers in decisions so that no one feels left out. *Everything indicates that you make your decisions quickly and don't listen to the doubts and lack of understanding coming from your subordinates, so you don't pick up on the reason for their uncertainty, either.* | | |
| 7 | | **Action:** Creating a shared understanding of what needs to be done and how, before you get the ball rolling. *Your subordinates say they are unable to tell what their roles are in the work they're supposed to do and they don't know what responsibilities they share in the team effort to find and implement solutions* | | |

*The actions listed above are statements taken directly from the original questionnaire.*

## What You Do Now

Now it is time for you and your coach to start putting together your Mental Scorecard. Looking at what you've learned about your leadership focus, how you are perceived by others, what your subordinates and the situation require, and the general focus requirements of your job, go through the questionnaire aimed at determining focus requirements located at the back of the book (Document 16).

You should list a number of leadership actions that you will carry out in practice over a period of 14 days. Once the two weeks are up, and you have carried out these actions, then you should evaluate if and how well you did so. If you feel that things went really well and that in the future you will be able to carry out a similar leadership action without having to make elaborate preparations, then give yourself two points. If not, give yourself minus two points. The ideal score is the number of situations/actions on your scorecard times two. If you have six actions on your scorecard, then your ideal score is 12. Once you have given yourself points for each action, then you can calculate your leadership handicap, which what you get when you add together the points you earned for your actions during the 14-day period minus your ideal score. To put it in another way, for each action that you do not carry out satisfactorily, give yourself minus two points and the sum of your minus points is equal to your leadership handicap. The goal is to achieve a handicap of zero (in golf, it's called playing at scratch, getting the ideal score for the course): in other words, to gain the ability to carry out all the actions on your scorecard in a satisfactory manner.

If you don't make scratch by the time the 14 days are up, then you start with the same scorecard, and it should contain at least two of the actions for which you did not give yourself one or two points. In practice, it is a good idea to continue with the exact same scorecard, i.e. with all the actions, also the ones you carried out and got two points for in the first round. If you do this, changing focus to take these leadership actions will become almost automatic. Alternatively, you could replace one or more of the actions you mastered during the 14-day period with new actions that you didn't have room for on your first scorecard. In other words, keep playing on the course (carrying out the actions on the scorecard) until you can play it at scratch (obtain your ideal score). Once you achieve this goal, then you play a new and slightly more difficult course, i.e. make a new scorecard with new actions on it, and play this new course until you obtain your ideal score again. Theoretically, you just could keep on going, doing new scorecards until you retire.

You can find out what leadership actions to put on your scorecard by employing a questionnaire at the back of this book (Document 16). You can photocopy the number you need. The starting point for you and your coach filling in the questionnaire is *"Based on what you know about and the experience you have with [name]'s leadership focus, how much more or less focus do you think he/she should have on the following:"* Diagram 19 shows an excerpt of this form, which allows you and your coach to go through each one of the statements that you and each person giving you feedback on your leadership focus have answered.

On the basis of the feedback you receive from your superior, your colleagues and your subordinates, you should now respond to the same statements, but only in an assessment as to whether you should focus more or less on the type of leadership that each individual statement represents. In the example in Diagram 19, the person filling in the scorecard responded to Statements 5 and 6 by putting an "X" under **Much More:**

*Formulating clear guidelines for your subordinates' responsibilities and work performance*
*Creating a work environment with room and time for being social and making small talk*

And to Statement 1:

*Helping and supporting subordinates who are in difficulty and/or have a hard time managing*

the reaction was an "X" under **Somewhat more.** There is an X under "OK" for four statements, i.e. those things the leader in question does not need to work with. To Statement 3, the respondent answered **Somewhat less:**

*Acting and being perceived as an active, energetic and goal-oriented leader*

| | Based on what you know about and the experience you have with _____ _____'s leadership focus, how much more or less focus do you think he/she should have on the following areas: | Much more | Somewhat more | No more or less | Somewhat less | Much less | Prioritization |
|---|---|---|---|---|---|---|---|
| 1 | Helping and supporting subordinates that have difficulty managing | | x | | | | |
| 2 | Organizing things so that subordinates can do their work thoroughly and systematically | | | x | | | |
| 3 | Acting and being perceived as an active, energetic and goal-oriented leader | | | | x | | |
| 4 | Leading the way when changes have to be made | | | x | | | |
| 5 | Formulating clear guidelines for responsibilities and work performance | x | | | | | |
| 6 | Creating a work environment with room and time for being social and making small talk | x | | | | | |
| 7 | Inspiring your subordinates to come up with creative solutions | | | x | | | |
| 8 | Ensuring that everyone always utilizes time and other resources efficiently and in a targeted manner. | | | x | | | |

The Leader's Mental Scorecard. © Finn Havaleschka.

Formulating clear guidelines has to do with Baser leadership. Creating an environment with room for workers to socialize and helping and supporting your subordinates is Integrator leadership. Not paying so much attention to whether you are seen to be an active, energetic and goal-oriented leader: that is being less focused on Results leadership. Thus the responses to the statements in Diagram 19 indicate a wish that the leader would move a little away from Results leadership towards Baser leadership while increasing his/her focus on Integrator leadership. This movement towards Baser and Integrator leadership can be illustrated as shown in Figure 48.

## Figure 48. The focus alternatives for the Results leader
### (The black profile)

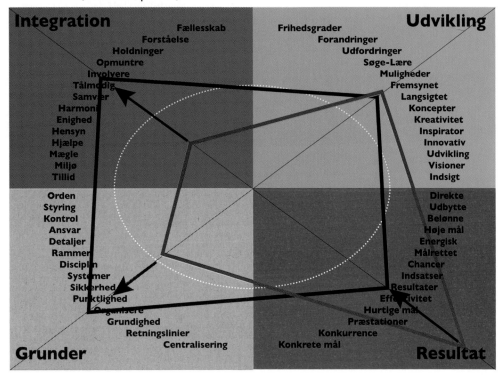

Once you have found the actions or areas you should practice, then draw that into the model. Take a photocopy of the model (Document 3, 12 or 13), draw your own profile on it and then add, as illustrated in Figure 48, a profile with the focus areas you should learn to include in your repertoire. There are no exact rules for calculating how far out into the corners your new "mental"

profile should go: that's completely up to you and your own perception. The most important reason for doing it at all is the awareness it creates about where you need to "move."

Naturally, there are limits to how many leadership actions you can include on one scorecard. Generally, I recommend using a maximum of six actions per scorecard. The number of actions must not be larger than the number you can realistically expect to be able to carry out. For this reason, once you have been through the entire questionnaire that tells you where your focus needs are, then you will have to prioritize, as you can see in the example in Diagram 20.

# Diagram 20. Focus actions and priorities for Claus Persson

**In your daily decisions and your role as a leader, I/we feel that the following is something you should consider:**

| # | | Much more | Somewhat more | Neither more nor less | Somewhat less | Much less | Priority |
|---|---|---|---|---|---|---|---|
| 1 | Helping and supporting subordinates who are in difficulty and/or have a hard time managing | | x | | | | 9 |
| 2 | Organizing things so that subordinates can do their work thoroughly and systematically | | | x | | | |
| 3 | Acting and being perceived as an active, energetic and goal-oriented leader | | | | | x | 5 |
| 4 | Leading the way when changes have to be made | | | x | | | |
| 5 | Formulating clear guidelines for responsibilities and work performance | x | | | | | 4 |
| 6 | Creating a work environment with room and time for being social and making small talk | x | | | | | 1 |
| 7 | Inspiring your subordinates to come up with creative solutions | | | x | | | |
| 8 | Ensuring that everyone always utilizes time and other resources efficiently and in a targeted manner | | | x | | | |
| 9 | Encouraging, praising, supporting and motivating all coworkers | x | | | | | 2 |
| 10 | Having systems so it's easy to see how far along people are in the work schedule/plans | | | x | | | |
| 11 | Leading the way in working efficiently and targeted | | | x | | | |
| 12 | Ensuring everyone has the space, facilities and opportunity to solve problems independently | | | x | | | |
| 13 | Making your decisions based on clear and certain facts | | x | | | | 8 |
| 14 | Knowing what the background, values and attitudes of your subordinates are | | | x | | | |
| 15 | Playing a vital role in the development of concepts and strategies | | | x | | | |
| 16 | Your people do not waste time, but concentrate on creating visible results and getting things done | | | x | | | |
| 17 | Mediating and unifying when different opinions and interests could cause conflict | | x | | | | 6 |
| 18 | Having systems that create structure, order and discipline in subordinates' activities | x | | | | | 3 |
| 19 | Ensuring that there is always a certain degree of competition among your subordinates | | | x | | | |
| 20 | Being a source of inspiration and creative partner for your subordinates | | | x | | | |
| 21 | Directing and monitoring important tasks until completion | | | x | | | |
| 22 | Creating a positive, open and trusting environment | | x | | | | 7 |
| 23 | Making long-term goals clear and comprehensible to everyone | | | x | | | |
| 24 | Being more direct, specific and definite if results fail to appear | | | x | | | |

# Diagram 21. Mental Scorecard for Claus Persson

| Sit. | Color | Focus, Calendar Weeks 43 and 44, 2004 | + | - |
|---|---|---|---|---|
| 1 | | **Action:** Creating a work environment with room and time for being social and making small talk. *You are too busy with your own work, and your own need to be social is limited.* <br>• Consider whether changes can be made in the layout and décor of the workplace that could promote a feeling of community. <br>• Spend 10-15 minutes a day going to see and talking with your subordinates. <br>• Consider whether you should hold an informal after-work meeting, e.g. every Friday. | | |
| | | Evaluate your ability to focus on and carry out this action. | | |
| 2 | | **Action:** Encouraging, praising, supporting and motivating all coworkers. *This is a bit connected with the first action. You aren't good enough at expressing your satisfaction.* <br>• Be aware that you need to give people praise and feedback. Remember the one-minute manager method! | | |
| | | Evaluate your ability to focus on and carry out this action. | | |
| 3 | | **Action:** Ensuring there are systems that create structure, order and discipline in subordinates' activities. *You have no difficulty living with chaos and still maintaining an overview, but several of your subordinates do.* <br>• Take the problem to your subordinates. You may want to let them make an analysis themselves and give you suggestions. | | |
| | | Evaluate your ability to focus on and carry out this action. | | |
| 4 | | **Action:** Formulating clear guidelines for responsibilities and work performance. *This is connected with Action 3.* <br>• Have a talk with each individual subordinate. The idea is that each one should have enough information and thus clearly understand what his/her responsibilities and duties are, that he/she can propose a description that you can discuss with him/her and come to an agreement on. | | |
| | | Evaluate your ability to focus on and carry out this action. | | |
| 5 | Reject | **Action:** Acting and being perceived as an active, energetic and goal-oriented leader. *You have a tendency to set goals that are too high. You have great ambitions, which is why you are most often way ahead of your subordinates, both in thought and action. When time after time you – consciously or unconsciously – allocate too little time to projects, people end up not taking your objectives and time schedules seriously.* <br>• Set realistic goals and discuss with your subordinates. Listen to them; let them help make the decisions. | | |
| | | Evaluate your ability to focus on and carry out this action. | | |
| 6 | | **Action:** Be aware of GU's need for feedback and trust. [GU is a subordinate of Claus'.]* <br>*You are losing GU. He is frustrated and ready to leave the organization because he doesn't get enough attention and trust.* <br>• Have a serious talk with him, and give him your frank assessment of his work and future in the organization. | | |
| | | Evaluate your ability to focus on and carry out this action. | | |
| | | **Results for the 14 days** | | |
| | | **Ideal Score (6 actions x 2 points)** | 12 | |
| | | **Your Mental Leadership Handicap** | | |

*This action is formulated on the basis of a conversation between the coach and the leaders subordinate, named GU.

The Leader's Mental Scorecard. © Finn Havaleschka.

The remarks in italics under each action description are the coach's remarks and reasons for including the action. The boldface type that follows indicates suggestions as to how the leader can carry out the action in practice. It is impossible to give more than general advice as to how the different types of actions can be carried out best. Everything depends on the situation, of course, and the people involved. To help you, included below is a list of questions you can ask for each of the four leadership areas, as a starting point for or as a prelude to writing the individual leadership actions on your own scorecard.

In general, Baser leadership is focusing on precision, order, control, systematics, checking, organization, planning, and making, knowing and following rules. Subordinates who have a personality that gives them a focus on the Gray area have corresponding needs that must be fulfilled. Baser subordinates prefer things to be predictable; they would rather not make decisions if they can't foresee or predict the consequences.

Thus Gray leadership actions are actions that require a specific analysis of these factors, i.e. purely intellectual and systematic logical thinking. To find out what kind of Gray leadership actions would be helpful to you, you should ask questions such as:

- What rules apply?
- Are there any formal systems?
- How is planning handled?
- Have clear boundaries or limits been set?
- Are there people who need more rules and/or instructions than others?
- Are there things that could/should be organized better?
- Are there time schedules to be followed?
- Are things communicated clearly and comprehensibly?
- Is there a need for drawings, graphs, models, checklists, etc.?
- In which of the four focus areas are each of your subordinates, and what does that say about their individual needs?

When you ask these questions, you will more or less automatically build up a list of Gray leadership actions: the practical things you need to focus on and how you need to do it. For example, are there clearly defined rules? Are such rules needed? How should they be worded and who should draft them? How should they be communicated?

Generally speaking, **Results leadership** requires taking specific leadership steps to achieve clearly defined goals within a specific short time frame and by utilizing certain resources. To find out what your Red leadership actions should be, you should ask yourself questions such as:

- Are there specific objectives?
- Does everyone know what these objectives are?
- Do my subordinates believe it is important to achieve these objectives?
- Do they know why it is important to achieve them?
- Do they know the larger picture of which their activities are part?
- Are the objectives realistic?
- Have standards for performance been defined?
- Does each subordinate know what is expected of him/her?
- Are there any reward systems in place?
- Are your subordinates motivated? Are they committed and enthusiastic?
- In which of the four focus areas are each of my subordinates, and what does that say about their individual needs?

When you ask these questions, you will more or less automatically find out what your Red leadership actions should be, the practical things you need to focus on, and how you need to do it.

To look at the next focus area, Integrator leadership requires a focus on understanding and patience and on making sure everyone feels like part of a community or team. You need to communicate objectives, concepts, strategies, means and methods, and make sure subordinates understand and appreciate them. To find out what your Blue leadership actions should be, you should ask yourself questions about the needs of each of your subordinates:

- Do meetings need to be held?
- Should we hold formal/informal discussions?
- Do they need more information?
- Should more attention be paid to each individual worker?
- What are their individual, more private needs?
- What would add to their motivation and job satisfaction?
- What motivates each of my subordinates?
- Do any of them have any special interests?
- Are there any conflicts of interest or anything like that?
- In which of the four focus areas are each of my subordinates to be found, and what does that say about their individual needs?

When you ask these questions, you will more or less automatically find out you're your Blue leadership actions should be: the practical things you need to focus on and how you need to do it.

And, to take the fourth focus area, **Development leadership** is about laying down strategies, innovation and determining what future concepts should be: long-term aspects. However, Development leadership also requires specific action and decisions that give coworkers an overview, promote worker creativity and their will to accept and possibly lead processes that create change. To find out what your Green leadership actions should be, you should ask yourself questions such as:

- Where do our current strategies, products, methods, etc. come from?
- What facts, theories, etc. are they based on?
- What was the basic idea?
- What does this basic idea look like today?
- What is necessary for changes to be made?
- How do we sell the ideas?
- Is it possible to get people enthusiastic about our visions?
- Are my subordinates allowed to work with some of these problems?
- Do we challenge people enough intellectually?
- Do we delegate enough work?
- Is it being delegated to the right people?
- In which of the four focus areas are each of my subordinates to be found, and what does that say about their individual needs?

The idea behind this list of questions is that when you and your coach try to answer them, it should help generate ideas as to how you can carry out the leadership actions you write down on your Mental Scorecard.

## Write Down Your Own Actions

**This is crucial!** If you go back to the last action listed on Claus' scorecard in Diagram 21 – "Be aware of GU's need for feedback and trust" – you will note that it is not taken directly from the questionnaire, but written on the basis of the observations the involved parties made during the process. They noted that Claus was losing one of his key workers for the simple reason that this person did not feel that Claus had confidence in him or showed him the necessary trust. From Claus' viewpoint, this was not true at all. The problem arose because Claus is partly in the Green and partly in the Red area of the model, while this person (GU) is in the Blue area, an area that Claus has very little focus on. This relationship is an example of what happens when a manager does not move his focus to the place where his worker has his focus. The example also illustrates the way you can define your own leadership actions independently of the questionnaire and look at specific things that you are currently having problems with.

## Involve Others in Defining Actions

Depending on the situation, your personality, your subordinates and the culture of the organization you work for, it is possible to involve others in determining what leadership actions you should write into your scorecard. If you want others to be involved, it is quite simple: give them the questionnaire entitled "Current Focus Needs" (Document 16 at the back of the book). Once this person – boss, colleague or subordinate – has filled in the sheet, you can have a talk with him/her and also ask if he/she has any practical ideas as to how the action or actions in question could be carried out. If you asked several people for feedback via the questionnaire, you can compare their ideas, e.g. to see how many have the same or similar ideas. This will give you an impression of how to prioritize your leadership actions. If you are a more open type of manager and work in an antiauthoritarian and open organizational culture, it might be productive to ask a group of your coworkers to fill in a questionnaire together. Once they do that, you can ask them why they point to the actions they did and how they think the leadership actions could be carried out in practice. In an open corporate culture, you might even be able to go so far as to allow the person or persons to give you points on your Mental Scorecard to reflect their observations as to whether you were able to change focus and carry out the actions on your scorecard.

Once you have selected the people you would like to have help you with your Mental Scorecard, and you have decided how you want them to help you, I would suggest you attempt to fill out the questionnaire yourself and write down the actions you think are appropriate on your scorecard. You will find the questionnaire (Document 16) at the back of the book, in the appendix. Do it before you move on to the next section below (the one entitled

"Mental and Practical Preparation"). Once you have found the actions you will be working with first and have written them onto your Mental Scorecard, then begin reading again, starting here.

## Mental and Practical Preparation

Your task now is to sit down with your coach and find out how you should perform the actions you have written on your Mental Scorecard. This is when the real work begins. It starts at the intellectual level, in a controlled mental and emotional process in which you imagine – also including feeling, seeing, hearing, taste and touch as much as you can – the processes and activities necessary for you to carry each leadership action through successfully. In this process, is incredibly important to remember that:

**All other things being equal, what you do not in advance imagine and add to your psychological world, you will have difficulty carrying out in practice in the real world.**

**On the other hand, the more you think, imagine, or put up on your internal television screen about how you will act in a certain way in certain situations, the greater the chances that you will be able to actually do so in reality.**

In other words, the idea is to plan ahead, imagining when and how you will carry out each leadership act and under what circumstances. Use the example of Blue leadership in Diagram 22 below as a starting point and an illustration of how you can plan the content of your own leadership actions.

## Diagram 22. Focus on Blue Leadership

| Sit. | Color | Focus, Calendar Weeks 17 and 18, 2004 | Points | |
|------|-------|----------------------------------------|:---:|:---:|
| | | | + | - |
| 7 | | **Action:** Creating a shared understanding of and motivation in connection with the work to be done. <br> *- Your subordinates have no clear idea of the roles they should play; they feel no joint responsibility and are generally not very motivated.* | 2 | |

The Leader's Mental Scorecard. © Finn Havaleschka.

This example shows a manager that needs to focus more on making sure everyone understands the work to be done and is motivated to do it. Questionnaire results, etc. show that subordinates lack a clear sense of what roles they are supposed to play; they feel no joint responsibility for its performance, and they do not generally feel especially motivated. If you were this manager, and you were in doubt as to how you could specifically correct the situation described, then you could start by answering the Integrator leadership questions I asked just above:

- Do meetings need to be held?
- Do we need to hold formal/informal discussions?
- Do they need more information?
- Should more attention be paid to each individual worker?
- Are there any specific individual, more private needs that should be taken into consideration?
- What would add to their motivation and job satisfaction?
- What motivates each of my subordinates?
- Do any of them have any special interests?
- In which of the four focus areas are each of my subordinates to be found, and what does that say about their individual needs?

On the basis of your answers to these questions, you could then make a plan, an outline of how you intended to carry out the action and achieve the goal of "creating a shared understanding of and motivation in connection with the work to be done." So put yourself in this leader's place now, and sit down with your coach and find the answers to questions such as whether you should call a formal meeting or can things be handled in more informal discussions? Do you need to talk with individual subordinates? Do they lack information, and, if so, what information do they need and how can you give it to them? Are there some people that need more attention than others? Can you think of anything general or specific that will motivate your coworkers? Are there coworkers that have any special interests or knowledge that you can involve in the process? If you know where individual subordinates are in the Focus Model, what does that then tell you about how you should communicate with and motivate them? The above example is simply intended to give you a methodology of finding your way to your own specific actions, i.e. the leadership actions you can and should carry out in order to achieve the goals you put on your own Mental Scorecard.

Once you have put the goals/actions you want to work on into your scorecard, and you know just how you want to carry them out, then comes the most important part. You now have to give yourself time alone to rehearse in your imagination how you are going to do these things. You have to be able to see, hear and feel the process. When you do it, remember the rules for mental training that I told you about in the first part of this book. Much of it is about having a positive attitude, about your basic approach to life, yourself and your fellow human beings. One thing you can do is take a quick look at the sayings about life that are on the inside of the back cover of this book. You might want to discuss them with your coach. Especially important is your attitude to others and your expectations with respect to their reactions. If you expect negative reactions, you'll get them. Think about the example I mentioned about Thorleif Krarup.

> *There was a great deal of dissatisfaction among the employees about various working conditions and decisions that had been made…. He listened; he understood; he explained things so people could understand them…. In spite of the harsh tone he was met with at the beginning, at no time did he take it personally, feel insulted, or try to defend himself. He explained, clarified things and listened to people's good ideas. The people at the meeting became involved in the process, and it became their project.*

The mistake that Thorleif *avoided* was to allow himself to be governed by negative expectations. If you expect that a certain subordinate will be standoffish and negative, then you have already adopted a mindset that will have you perceiving all questions from this person as negative and unconstructive, as if his/her questions are only intended to sabotage your good intentions. At the same time, your answers will reflect your expectations, both in content and tone. Remember also that the first thing this person will register is *not* what you say, your ideas or your intentions, but the attitude you radiate both physically and mentally. For this reason, it is incredibly important that you include your attitude when you are making your mental preparations:

try to visualize yourself radiating a positive attitude. If your intention is positive and constructive, you should visualize yourself acting in a positive and constructive fashion, with an open and trusting attitude.

It may sound like pop psychology, but there is good reason to take it seriously. To act in a positive and constructive manner and so that others see you as such, it is necessary for you to be able to imagine yourself act in a positive and constructive manner. If it is difficult for you to do so, then remember that the only way to really get rid of a negative or nonconstructive thought is to replace it with a different thought. It is not enough to admonish yourself and tell yourself to be positive! Before the trick of substituting another thought for the negative thought can work, the substitute thought has to contain more energy than the thought you are attempting to push away. You probably know the situation from your everyday life. Sometimes you can be a bit down, pessimistic: things are difficult and going in the wrong direction. It can be difficult to pull yourself up by your bootstraps. What works best is if something completely different happens, something sudden and unplanned: an order comes in unexpectedly, unexpected good news, a smile or someone laughing. This kind of thing brings with it positive energy. Your senses pick up on these experiences and transform them into energy and affect your mood. Of course, we don't think about the biochemical processes that these experiences trigger and push the negative energy away, but that's what actually happens.

The point is that we are not dependent of our surroundings or external stimuli to trigger our emotions: we do it all the time, unconsciously and completely independent of other people. If you are looking forward to something, it makes you happy. So what came first: what you were looking forward to or the happiness you felt in anticipating it? If you think that something is very wrong, then your mood changes to accommodate that thought, and you act accordingly. You create energy on the basis of expectation, not just on the basis of facts. It is this mechanism – the connection between your thoughts, the biochemical processes and your mood – that you must learn to control.

One way is to sit down, close your eyes and imagine how you and the people involved go through a process accompanied by openness, constructive questions, trust and smiles. Imagine, feel, or try to create the feeling it would involve to be a part of that process: imagine the smiles, the laughing and positive remarks. Draw on how you felt in good experiences past: how you felt when you fell in love, when you were a part of something big, something that overwhelmed you with happiness. Think of these things and hold onto that feeling. Bring that feeling into your mind, into your imagination, and you will see that it is difficult to hold onto that negative or unconstructive thought. Finally, when you are planning the actions you want to carry out, and you run through the process in your mind, showing it on your inner movie screen, then think of Maslow's description of a whole self: a person who lives and acts in accordance with his/her inner nature. When you plan your leadership actions, try to:

1. Make your choices independently of other people's opinions and their positive or negative expectations. Remember that you are not a leader just to impress other people.
2. Focus on the process, live in it, and be a part of it.
3. See and understand that the results of your choices and what you do are feedback on the process, i.e. on why you got the results you did, and adjust your next decision and your behavior accordingly.

And if you are in doubt as to whether you are on the right path, then follow Maslow's advice and ask yourself,

If I do this, will it bring me peace of mind?

I wish you the best of luck.

# About communication and four roads to happiness

Four people walk about seeking happiness in each their separate corners of the world. Perhaps a few of them are in fact more occupied by protecting themselves against unhappiness. However that may be, they each have their own ideas as to how and what it takes to live happily. As no one truly can be happy alone, without having anyone to share with, they each stand in their corners trying to persuade the others to come to their corner, where they will find happiness together.

However this is not easily done. None of them are willing to leave their own safe and secure corner of the world in order to seek happiness in an unknown corner. The advantage of this conviction is that it provides stability in life, the organization, at work and at home with one's family. The disadvantage however, is that it cause stagnation.

You can have different opinions about this, though it seems that all agree that **we are all masters of our own destiny.**

# About Communication and Four Roads to Happiness

*(Start by reading the text in the Developer corner, then the text in the Baser corner, then the text in the Integrator corner and finally in the Result corner).*

## ■ Integrator happiness

"No, hey, guys, come up here! It's cozy; we have a nice time here; we care about each other; we talk about things. We don't exclude anyone; we stick together. Together we find happiness!"

## ■ Baser happiness

"Uh, no … it seems chaotic up there in the Green corner. Come to my corner! Things are safe and secure here; we always have enough to pay the rent; we don't get in over our heads; we keep the wolf away from the door!"

The Leader's Mental Scorecard. © Finn Havaleschka.

242

## Developer happiness

"Where are you at, guys? Come up here! You'll get insight and an overview. We help and inspire each other – this is where we make the future! This is the way to happiness!"

## Result happiness

Hey, guys, c'mon to my corner! You can talk, make rules and be innovative, but we make the results. That's what keeps this organization alive! We compete and have fun. Live life while you can – that's the way to happiness!"

The Leader's Mental Scorecard. © Finn Havaleschka.

# Appendix

Questionnaires and forms to copy and complete[45]

---

[45] The questionnaires, models, figures and schemes published in this book are meant to be used by the owner of this book only. Copying and use of the materials for professional and commercial reasons are strictly against the law. If you like to use the materials in professional or commercial activities and for larger groups, you are welcome to contact Garuda or the author. See contact details on the last page.

## Document 1: The Leadership Profile personal questionnaire[46]

The questionnaire is on the next page. You can respond to each of the 24 statements by indicating what you focus on in your daily work, and you do that by marking whether you believe that the subject matter of each statement is very important, fairly important, neutral, less important or not important. See the following example.

| © Garuda Research Institute - info@garudahr.com<br><br>*In my daily decisions and in my role as a manager, I believe the following is:* | Very important | Fairly important | Neutral | Less important | Not important |
|---|:---:|:---:|:---:|:---:|:---:|
| Helping and supporting others who are in difficulty and/or have a hard time managing | | | | | x |
| Organizing things so that subordinates can do their jobs thoroughly and systematically | | | x | | |
| Acting and being perceived as an active, energetic and goal-oriented leader | x | | | | |
| Leading the way when changes have to be made | | | | x | |

*An X under "Neutral" means "I don't know, I'm not sure, haven't thought about it"*

Do not rank the different statements; simply answer each one based on how you see yourself in acting in your daily work life, i.e. what you focus the most on as a manager, as well as what you do not focus so much on. You should be able to answer most statements right away and spontaneously, without thinking too much about it first, and doing so will also provide the best basis for the work you will do afterwards. If you are in doubt, remember that the statements are about your leadership focus only.

---

[46] Please note that this questionnaire and the other questionnaires in the book are shorter versions than the original questionnaires installed in the software used by Garuda and other HR consultants and coaches. In practice, this means that the profile you will work with, stemming as it does from the "little questionnaire," will not necessarily be exactly the same as if you use the original questionnaire, which contains almost three times as many statements, and therefore will be more reliable. With a smaller number of questions compared to a larger number the profile may change a bit depending on the situation you are in when you complete the questionnaire.

The Leader's Mental Scorecard. © Finn Havaleschka.

# Document 1

| | © Garuda Research Institute - info@garudahr.com<br><br>***In my daily decisions and in my role as a leader, I believe the following is:*** | Very important | Fairly important | Neutral | Less important | Not important |
|---|---|---|---|---|---|---|
| 1 | Helping and supporting others who are in difficulty and/or have a hard time managing | | | | | |
| 2 | Organizing things so that subordinates can do their jobs thoroughly and systematically | | | | | |
| 3 | Acting and being perceived as an active, energetic and goal-oriented leader | | | | | |
| 4 | Leading the way when changes have to be made | | | | | |
| 5 | Formulating clear guidelines for responsibility and work performance | | | | | |
| 6 | Creating a work environment with room and time for being social and making small talk | | | | | |
| 7 | Inspiring subordinates to come up with creative solutions | | | | | |
| 8 | Ensuring that everyone always utilizes time and other resources efficiently and in a targeted manner | | | | | |
| 9 | Encouraging, praising, supporting and motivating all coworkers | | | | | |
| 10 | Having systems so it's easy to see how far along people are in the work schedule/plans | | | | | |
| 11 | Leading the way in working efficiently and targeted | | | | | |
| 12 | Ensuring everyone has the space, facilities and opportunity to solve problems independently | | | | | |
| 13 | Making my decisions based on clear and certain facts | | | | | |
| 14 | Knowing what the background, values and attitudes of my subordinates are | | | | | |
| 15 | Playing a vital role in the development of concepts and strategies | | | | | |
| 16 | That people do not waste time, but concentrate on creating visible results and getting things done | | | | | |
| 17 | Mediating and unifying when different opinions and interests could cause conflict | | | | | |
| 18 | Having systems that create structure, order and discipline in subordinates' activities | | | | | |
| 19 | Ensuring that there is always a certain degree of competition among subordinates | | | | | |
| 20 | Being a source of inspiration and creative partner for subordinates | | | | | |
| 21 | Directing and monitoring important tasks until completion | | | | | |
| 22 | Creating a positive, open and trusting environment | | | | | |
| 23 | Making long-term goals clear and comprehensible to everyone | | | | | |
| 24 | Being more direct, specific and definite if results fail to appear | | | | | |

The Leader's Mental Scorecard. © Finn Havaleschka.

## Document 2: Calculating Your Score

Once you have indicated your response to all 24 statements, you may add your points together. Do this by transferring your answers to the table below. If you replied *Very important* to the first statement in the questionnaire, then circle the number 4 in the *Very important* column in the table below and write 4 in the blank field to the right of the equal sign, under *Integrator,* and so on. Then accumulate the total score for each area and write the result in the column.

| © Garuda Research Institute - info@garudahr.com | Very important | Fairly important | Neutral | Less important | Not important | | Integrator | Baser | Results | Development |
|---|---|---|---|---|---|---|---|---|---|---|
| Integrator focus | 4 | 2 | 0 | -2 | -4 | = | | | | |
| Baser focus | 4 | 2 | 0 | -2 | -4 | = | | | | |
| Results focus | 4 | 2 | 0 | -2 | -4 | = | | | | |
| Development focus | 4 | 2 | 0 | -2 | -4 | = | | | | |
| Baser focus | 4 | 2 | 0 | -2 | -4 | = | | | | |
| Integrator focus | 4 | 2 | 0 | -2 | -4 | = | | | | |
| Development focus | 4 | 2 | 0 | -2 | -4 | = | | | | |
| Results focus | 4 | 2 | 0 | -2 | -4 | = | | | | |
| Integrator focus | 4 | 2 | 0 | -2 | -4 | = | | | | |
| Baser focus | 4 | 2 | 0 | -2 | -4 | = | | | | |
| Results focus | 4 | 2 | 0 | -2 | -4 | = | | | | |
| Development focus | 4 | 2 | 0 | -2 | -4 | = | | | | |
| Baser focus | 4 | 2 | 0 | -2 | -4 | = | | | | |
| Integrator focus | 4 | 2 | 0 | -2 | -4 | = | | | | |
| Development focus | 4 | 2 | 0 | -2 | -4 | = | | | | |
| Results focus | 4 | 2 | 0 | -2 | -4 | = | | | | |
| Integrator focus | 4 | 2 | 0 | -2 | -4 | = | | | | |
| Baser focus | 4 | 2 | 0 | -2 | -4 | = | | | | |
| Results focus | 4 | 2 | 0 | -2 | -4 | = | | | | |
| Development focus | 4 | 2 | 0 | -2 | -4 | = | | | | |
| Baser focus | 4 | 2 | 0 | -2 | -4 | = | | | | |
| Integrator focus | 4 | 2 | 0 | -2 | -4 | = | | | | |
| Development focus | 4 | 2 | 0 | -2 | -4 | = | | | | |
| Results focus | 4 | 2 | 0 | -2 | -4 | = | | | | |
| **Integrator Points** | | | | | Total | | | | | |
| **Baser Points** | | | | | Total | | | | | |
| **Results Points** | | | | | Total | | | | | |
| **Development Points** | | | | | Total | | | | | |

The Leader's Mental Scorecard. © Finn Havaleschka.

# Document 3: Drawing Your Profile

Please note that a score of 24 (+24) should be indicated in the outer end of a corner, and a score of minus 24 (-24) is close to the middle of the Focus Model. Mark your scores on the diagonal axes, draw lines between them to connect the marks, and you will have your profile.

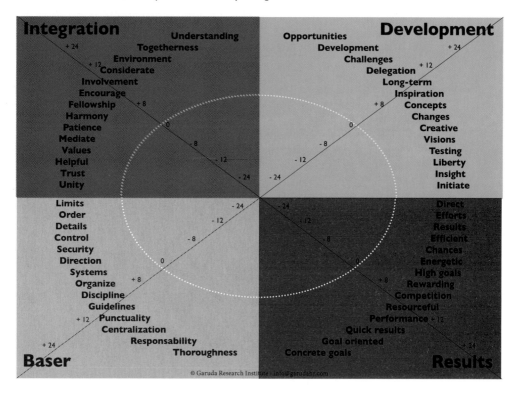

© Garuda Research Institute - info@garudahr.com

For a better overview, we recommend you also draw your Leadership Profile in the model figure 32 on page 143. You need it in sight when you are working with the exercise.

## Document 4: Main Type Descriptions

Baser leaders attach a great deal of importance to thoroughness and systematism and thus to creating frameworks and systems to lay the foundation for a structured, order-oriented and disciplined effort. As a result, Baser leaders believe it is important to lay down clear guidelines for the allocation of tasks and responsibilities.

Baser leaders prefer to make decisions based on clear and certain facts, and will tend to hold back if there is any uncertainty in the decision-making process. Finding solutions to new and unknown problems or issues are not left to or handed over to others. Most tasks are pursued to the end and in nearly every detail.

Control, organize, accuracy, facts, systematism, order, details and discipline are therefore key words for a Baser leader's mental approach to his role as a manager.

A disadvantage of this approach is that subordinates may be restricted or feel limited in their independence. Rule orientation, guidelines and centralization may dominate, leading to limited participation, involvement and desire to take responsibility. Under such circumstances, there is a risk that many subordinates react with a degree of passivity and indifference to daily work.

Results leaders emphasize everyone making a targeted and goal-oriented effort. It is vital to them that everyone always utilizes their resources and time fully and efficiently to achieve indisputable results. Results leaders will most often view competition, both internal and external, as an excellent motivating factor.

Results leaders are happy to lead the way in the pursuit of results, and they set specific and high goals for themselves and others. Results leader also emphasize hiring and rewarding goal-oriented employees. Results leaders are direct and straightforward people that have no patience with excuses and irrelevance.

Thus goals, visible results, energetic, active, goal orientation, impatience, efficiency, persistence, performance are key words in Results leaders' mental approach to their role as managers.

A disadvantage of this approach to management may be that subordinates easily feel pressured, feeling that the demands on them in their daily work are high and perhaps unobtainable. As a result, subordinates may feel stressed and discontented, that they are not listened to, or that no consideration is taken of the individual competencies and wishes.

Integrator leaders attach great importance to providing encouragement and support to their subordinates and take into consideration each person's values, viewpoints and opinions. Integrator leaders always try to be open, trusting, positive, patient and fair, and try to ensure that there is consensus regarding decisions.

Integrator leaders believe it is important to create an environment in which there is room for dialog, and they avoid conflict and disagreements. They want everyone to work together and share responsibility, and everyone is included in the decision-making process so no one feels left out.

Social togetherness, encouragement, support, praise, trust, consensus, fellowship, avoiding conflicts, justice, patience and tolerance are thus the key words that describe Integrator leaders's approach to their role as managers.

A disadvantage of this approach to management may be that subordinates may feel there is too much talking and discussion and not enough consistency. Integrator leaders try to treat everyone as equal, include everyone in the decision-making process, seek consensus and avoid making decisions that may lead to conflict or have the opposite effect of what was intended. Subordinates may become indifferent because as they do not see consistency or receive direction.

Development leaders want to be out ahead of the pack; work with long-term perspectives; develop general concepts and strategies, visions and ideas; find creative solutions; and test, discuss and experiment with new opportunities.

Normally, Development leaders feel it is extremely important to inspire and encourage their subordinates to take on challenges and to be proactive and forward-looking. This also means that their subordinates have a considerable degree of freedom and room to try out their own ideas and make independent decisions.

Change, creative solutions, new opportunities, concepts, visions, long-term goals, experiments, freedom, entrustment and independence are thus key words in describing the approach Development leaders take to their role as a manager.

A disadvantage of this approach to management may be that the subordinates lack limits and more specific and short-term objectives to aim for. Focusing on visions, new concepts and ideas can, for some workers, lead to insecurity in their everyday work life. Change – both real change and change only talked about – happens too quickly for some people, and this can make some workers feel insecure about their future, their place, and what they will be doing tomorrow.

## Document 5: Selected Type Descriptions

**Selection of the Baser role** may, in addition to what is mentioned above, limit subordinates' independence. Rule orientation, guidelines and centralization may dominate and limit the possibility of participation, involvement and desire to share responsibility. Under such circumstances, there is a risk that many subordinates will react with some degree of passivity and indifference to daily tasks.

**Selection of the Results role** may also mean that subordinates easily feel pressured because great demands – perhaps impossible ones – are made on them in their daily work. One consequence may be workers who feel stressed and dissatisfied who do not feel that they are being listened to, or that no consideration is shown to individual worker competencies and desires.

**Selection of the Integrator role** may, in addition to what is mentioned above, imply that subordinates feel that there is too much talk and discussion and not enough consistency. Integrator leaders' efforts to treat everyone as equals, include everyone in the decision-making process, seek consensus and avoid making decisions that may lead to conflict, can have the opposite effect than what was intended. The employees may become indifferent, as they do not experience consistency and direction.

**Selection of the Development role** may, in addition to what is mentioned above, imply that this leader's subordinates need structure as well as more specific and short-term goals to work towards. Focusing on new visions, new concepts, ideas and experiments may lead to insecurity in their everyday work life. Both real and the merely suggested changes happen too quickly, which may cause insecurity in some subordinates about their future, their place and what they will be doing tomorrow.

# Document 6: Deselected Type Descriptions

**Deselection of the Baser role** may imply that your subordinates feel insecure about task allocation, responsibility and the framework for their efforts. The framework for what is allowed and what is not, with or without permission, becomes unclear and may cause insecurity and a lack of ability or will to shoulder responsibility.

**Deselection of the Results role** may suggest that the employees tend to go their own way and set op goals and standards for their performance and efforts. Lack of precision about goals and objectives and the absence of reward may cause some degree of indifference, uninvolvement and the disclaiming of responsibility.

**Deselection of the Integrator role** may mean that subordinates go their own way and pursue their own goals without showing consideration towards other people because there is no sense of team spirit and thus no feeling of responsibility toward others and the group. In such circumstances, there is no motivation to help others, and in the worst-case scenario, each worker or group isolates themselves, which again may lay the foundation for conflict and poor teamwork.

**Deselection of the Development role** may imply that it is difficult for the employees to see themselves and their efforts in the overall picture. Under such circumstances, this may lead to a sense of emptiness and perhaps indifference, as the efforts put forth to achieve goals and the purpose of demands do not make sense and are not visible.

## Document 7: Mirror Profile: Questionnaire for Your Superior

The purpose of this Mirror Profile is to function as an introduction to a dialog about our perception of what a manager does or does not attach importance to in his daily management work. Your task now is to look at and respond to each of the statements on the basis of your experience with (name): _____'s ways of functioning in daily work.

| | © Garuda Research Institute - info@garudahr.com<br><br>**As this person's superior, my experience is that, in his/her role as leader and in daily decisions he/she believes the following to be:** | *Very important* | *Fairly important* | *Neutral* | *Less important* | *Not important* |
|---|---|---|---|---|---|---|
| 1 | Helping and supporting others who are in difficulty and/or have a hard time managing | | | | | |
| 2 | Organizing things so that subordinates can do their jobs thoroughly and systematically | | | | | |
| 3 | Acting and being perceived as an active, energetic and goal-oriented leader | | | | | |
| 4 | Leading the way when changes have to be made | | | | | |
| 5 | Formulating clear guidelines for subordinates' responsibilities and work performance | | | | | |
| 6 | Creating a job environment with room and time for being social and making small talk | | | | | |
| 7 | Inspiring subordinates to come up with creative solutions | | | | | |
| 8 | Ensuring that everyone always utilizes time and other resources efficiently and in a targeted manner | | | | | |
| 9 | Encouraging, praising, supporting and motivating all coworkers | | | | | |
| 10 | Having systems so it's easy to see how far along people are in the work schedule/plans | | | | | |
| 11 | Leading the way in working efficiently and targeted | | | | | |
| 12 | Ensuring subordinates have the space, facilities and opportunity to solve problems independently | | | | | |
| 13 | Making decisions based on clear and certain facts | | | | | |
| 14 | Knowing what the background, values and attitudes of subordinates are | | | | | |
| 15 | Playing a vital role in the development of concepts and strategies | | | | | |
| 16 | People do not waste time, but concentrate on creating visible results and getting things done | | | | | |
| 17 | Mediating and unifying when different opinions and interests could cause conflict | | | | | |
| 18 | Having systems that create structure, order and discipline in subordinates' activities | | | | | |
| 19 | Ensuring that there is always a certain degree of competition among subordinates | | | | | |
| 20 | Being a source of inspiration and creative partner for subordinates | | | | | |
| 21 | Directing and monitoring important tasks until completion | | | | | |
| 22 | Creating a positive, open and trusting environment | | | | | |
| 23 | Making long-term goals clear and comprehensible to everyone | | | | | |
| 24 | Being more direct, concrete and definite if results fail to appear | | | | | |

The Leader's Mental Scorecard. © Finn Havaleschka.

## Document 8: Mirror Profile: Questionnaire for Your Colleagues

The purpose of this Mirror Profile is to function as an introduction to a dialog about our perception of what a manager does or does not attach importance to in his daily management work. Your task now is to look at and respond to each of the statements on the basis of your experience with (name)_____'s ways of functioning in daily life at work.

| | © Garuda Research Institute - info@garudahr.com <br><br> *As this person's colleague, my experience is that he/she in the role as manger and in daily decisions believes the following to be:* | Very important | Fairly important | Neutral | Less important | Not important |
|---|---|---|---|---|---|---|
| 1 | Helping and supporting others who are in difficulty and/or have a hard time managing | | | | | |
| 2 | Organizing things so that subordinates can do their jobs thoroughly and systematically | | | | | |
| 3 | Acting and being perceived as an active, energetic and goal-oriented leader | | | | | |
| 4 | Leading the way when changes have to be made | | | | | |
| 5 | Formulating clear guidelines for subordinates' responsibilities and work performance | | | | | |
| 6 | Creating a work environment with room and time for being social and making small talk | | | | | |
| 7 | Inspiring subordinates to come up with creative solutions | | | | | |
| 8 | Ensuring that everyone always utilizes time and other resources efficiently and in a targeted manner | | | | | |
| 9 | Encouraging, praising, supporting and motivating all coworkers | | | | | |
| 10 | Having systems so it's easy to see how far along people are in the work schedule/plans | | | | | |
| 11 | Leading the way in working efficiently and targeted | | | | | |
| 12 | Ensuring subordinates have the space, facilities and opportunity to solve problems independently | | | | | |
| 13 | Making decisions based on clear and certain facts | | | | | |
| 14 | Knowing what the background, values and attitudes of your subordinates are | | | | | |
| 15 | Playing a vital role in the development of concepts and strategies | | | | | |
| 16 | People do not waste time, but concentrate on creating visible results and getting things done | | | | | |
| 17 | Mediating and unifying when different opinions and interests could cause conflict | | | | | |
| 18 | Having systems that create structure, order and discipline in subordinates' activities | | | | | |
| 19 | Ensuring that there is always a certain degree of competition among subordinates | | | | | |
| 20 | Being a source of inspiration and creative partner for subordinates | | | | | |
| 21 | Directing and monitoring important tasks until completion | | | | | |
| 22 | Creating a positive, open and trusting environment | | | | | |
| 23 | Making long-term goals clear and comprehensible to everyone | | | | | |
| 24 | Being more direct, concrete and definite if results fail to appear | | | | | |

The Leader's Mental Scorecard. © Finn Havaleschka.

## Document 9: Mirror Profile: Questionnaire for Your Subordinates

The purpose of this Mirror Profile is to function as an introduction to a dialog about our perception of what this manager does or does not attach importance to in his daily management work. Your task now is to look at and respond to each of the statements on the basis of your experience with _____'s ways of functioning in daily life at work.

| | © Garuda Research Institute - info@garudahr.com<br><br>*As employee, I experience that my manager believes the following to be:* | Very important | Fairly important | Neutral | Less important | Not important |
|---|---|---|---|---|---|---|
| 1 | Helping and supporting me if I have difficulty or a hard time living up to requirements | | | | | |
| 2 | Organizing things so I can do my job thoroughly and systematically | | | | | |
| 3 | Acting and being perceived as an active, energetic and goal-oriented leader | | | | | |
| 4 | Leading the way when changes have to be made | | | | | |
| 5 | Formulating clear guidelines for my responsibilities and work performance | | | | | |
| 6 | Creating a work environment with room and time for being social and making small talk | | | | | |
| 7 | Inspiring me to come up with creative solutions | | | | | |
| 8 | Ensuring that I always use my time and other resources efficiently and in a targeted manner | | | | | |
| 9 | Encouraging, praising, supporting and motivating me | | | | | |
| 10 | Having systems so it's easy to see how far along I am in the work schedule/plans | | | | | |
| 11 | Leading the way in working efficiently and targeted | | | | | |
| 12 | Ensuring that I have the space, facilities and opportunity to solve problems independently | | | | | |
| 13 | Making decisions based on clear and certain facts | | | | | |
| 14 | Knowing what my background, values and attitudes are | | | | | |
| 15 | Playing a vital role in the development of general concepts and strategies | | | | | |
| 16 | I do not waste time, but concentrate on creating visible results and getting things done | | | | | |
| 17 | Mediating and unifying when different opinions and interests could cause conflict | | | | | |
| 18 | Having systems that create structure, order and discipline in our activities | | | | | |
| 19 | Ensuring that there is always a certain degree of competition among us subordinates | | | | | |
| 20 | Being a source of inspiration and creative partner for me | | | | | |
| 21 | Directing and monitoring important tasks until completion | | | | | |
| 22 | He/she maintains a positive, open and trusting attitude towards me and what I do | | | | | |
| 23 | Making long-term goals clear and comprehensible to me | | | | | |
| 24 | He/she is more direct, concrete and definite if I do not get results | | | | | |

The Leader's Mental Scorecard. © Finn Havaleschka.

## Document 10: Calculating Your Scores

When the questionnaires have been completed and returned, you can add the points together. Begin by photocopying the table on the opposite page. Then transfer the statements from the individual questionnaires to each table, as you did when creating your personal profile. If necessary, go back and see how.

| | Very important | Fairly important | Neutral | Less important | Not important | | Integrator | Baser | Result | Development |
|---|---|---|---|---|---|---|---|---|---|---|
| Integrator focus | 4 | 2 | 0 | -2 | -4 | = | | | | |
| Baser focus | 4 | 2 | 0 | -2 | -4 | = | | | | |
| Results focus | 4 | 2 | 0 | -2 | -4 | = | | | | |
| Development focus | 4 | 2 | 0 | -2 | -4 | = | | | | |
| Baser focus | 4 | 2 | 0 | -2 | -4 | = | | | | |
| Integrator focus | 4 | 2 | 0 | -2 | -4 | = | | | | |
| Development focus | 4 | 2 | 0 | -2 | -4 | = | | | | |
| Results focus | 4 | 2 | 0 | -2 | -4 | = | | | | |
| Integrator focus | 4 | 2 | 0 | -2 | -4 | = | | | | |
| Baser focus | 4 | 2 | 0 | -2 | -4 | = | | | | |
| Results focus | 4 | 2 | 0 | -2 | -4 | = | | | | |
| Development focus | 4 | 2 | 0 | -2 | -4 | = | | | | |
| Baser focus | 4 | 2 | 0 | -2 | -4 | = | | | | |
| Integrator focus | 4 | 2 | 0 | -2 | -4 | = | | | | |
| Development focus | 4 | 2 | 0 | -2 | -4 | = | | | | |
| Results focus | 4 | 2 | 0 | -2 | -4 | = | | | | |
| Integrator focus | 4 | 2 | 0 | -2 | -4 | = | | | | |
| Baser focus | 4 | 2 | 0 | -2 | -4 | = | | | | |
| Results focus | 4 | 2 | 0 | -2 | -4 | = | | | | |
| Development focus | 4 | 2 | 0 | -2 | -4 | = | | | | |
| Baser focus | 4 | 2 | 0 | -2 | -4 | = | | | | |
| Integrator focus | 4 | 2 | 0 | -2 | -4 | = | | | | |
| Development focus | 4 | 2 | 0 | -2 | -4 | = | | | | |
| Results focus | 4 | 2 | 0 | -2 | -4 | = | | | | |
| **Integrator Points** | | | | | Total | | | | | |
| **Baser Points** | | | | | Total | | | | | |
| **Results Points** | | | | | Total | | | | | |
| **Development Points** | | | | | Total | | | | | |

The Leader's Mental Scorecard. © Finn Havaleschka.

## Document 11: Drawing Mirror Profiles

You are now ready to draw the Mirror Profiles. Please note that a score of 24 (+24) should be indicated in the outer end of a corner, and a score of minus 24 (-24) is close to the middle of the Focus Model. Mark your scores on the diagonal axes, draw lines between them to connect the marks, and you will have your profile. We recommend that you do not draw these profiles in below, but take photocopies of the figure below as needed instead. It is a good idea to draw each Mirror Profile on a separate copy as well as in the model Figure 32, 33 and 34 on page 94 and 95. You will need the profiles on separate sheets when you are going to discuss the profile with your 360-degree respondents.

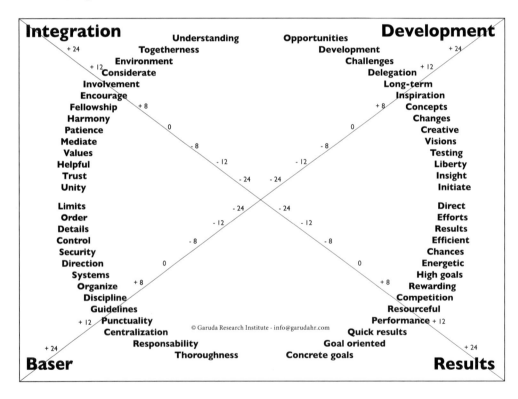

The Leader's Mental Scorecard. © Finn Havaleschka.

Document 12: Focus Model for Photocopying

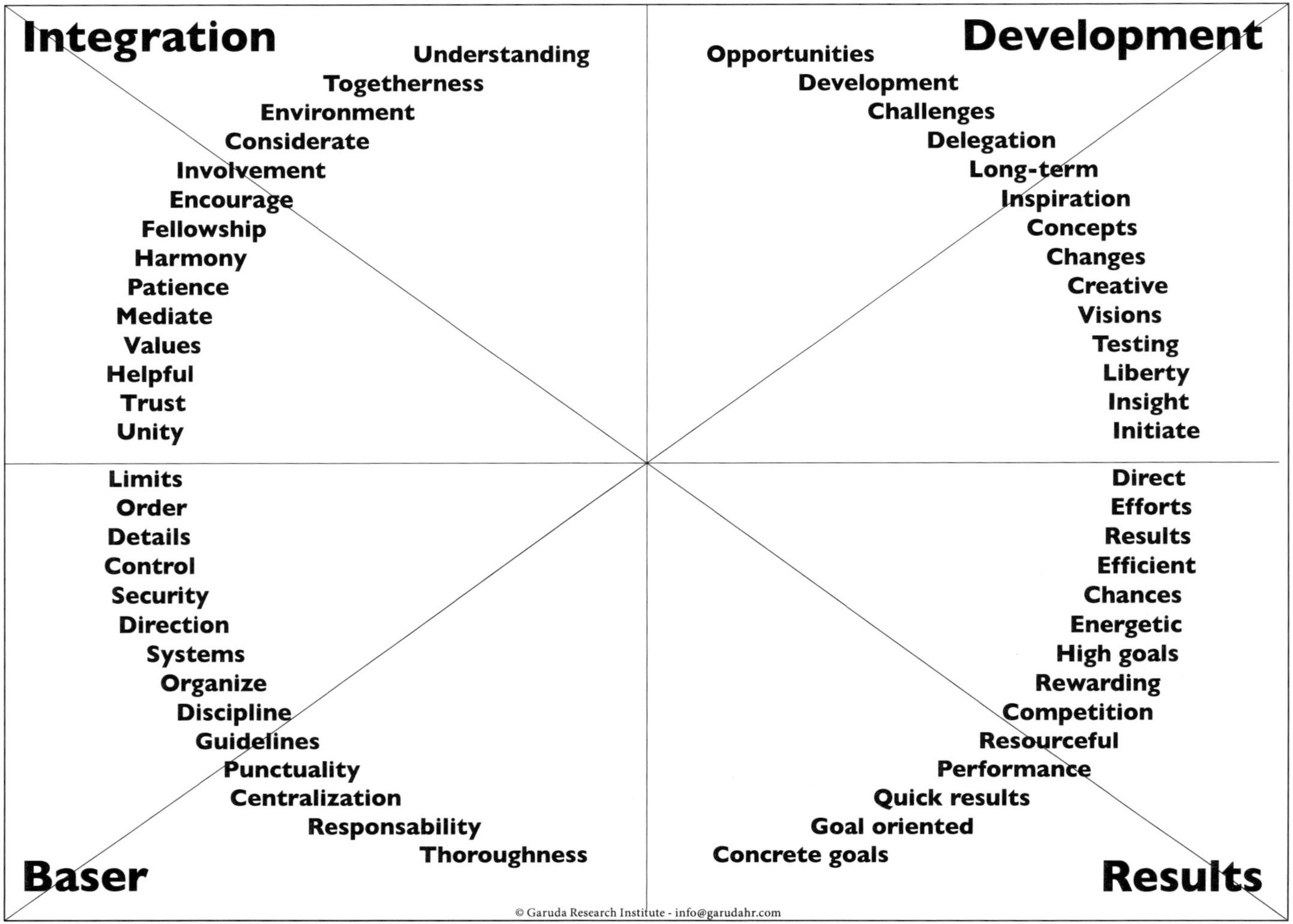

# Development

## Integration

Understanding
Togetherness
Environment
Considerate
Involvement
Encourage
Fellowship
Harmony
Patience
Mediate
Values
Helpful
Trust
Unity

Opportunities
Development
Challenges
Delegation
Long-term
Inspiration
Concepts
Changes
Creative
Visions
Testing
Liberty
Insight
Initiate

# Results

Direct
Efforts
Results
Efficient
Chances
Energetic
High goals
Rewarding
Competition
Resourceful
Performance
Quick results
Goal oriented
Concrete goals

Limits
Order
Details
Control
Security
Direction
Systems
Organize
Discipline
Guidelines
Punctuality
Centralization
Responsability
Thoroughness

# Baser

The Leader's Mental Scorecard. © Finn Havaleschka.

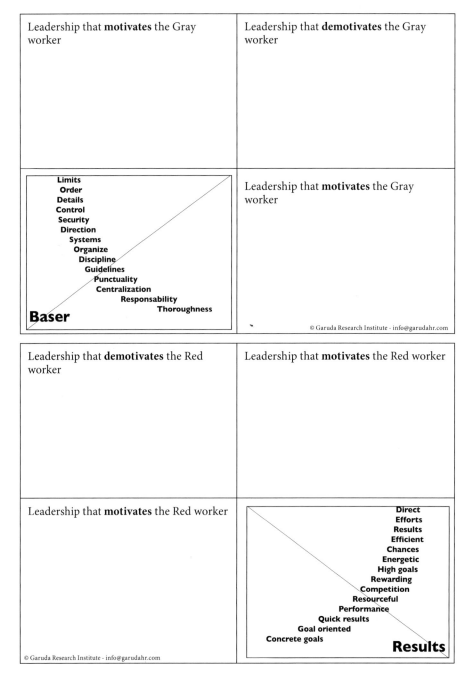

| Leadership that **motivates** the Gray worker | Leadership that **demotivates** the Gray worker |
|---|---|
| **Limits**<br>**Order**<br>**Details**<br>**Control**<br>**Security**<br>**Direction**<br>**Systems**<br>**Organize**<br>**Discipline**<br>**Guidelines**<br>**Punctuality**<br>**Centralization**<br>**Responsability**<br>**Thoroughness**<br>**Baser** | Leadership that **motivates** the Gray worker<br><br>© Garuda Research Institute - info@garudahr.com |
| Leadership that **demotivates** the Red worker | Leadership that **motivates** the Red worker |
| Leadership that **motivates** the Red worker<br><br>© Garuda Research Institute - info@garudahr.com | **Direct**<br>**Efforts**<br>**Results**<br>**Efficient**<br>**Chances**<br>**Energetic**<br>**High goals**<br>**Rewarding**<br>**Competition**<br>**Resourceful**<br>**Performance**<br>**Quick results**<br>**Goal oriented**<br>**Concrete goals**<br>**Results** |

The Leader's Mental Scorecard. © Finn Havaleschka.

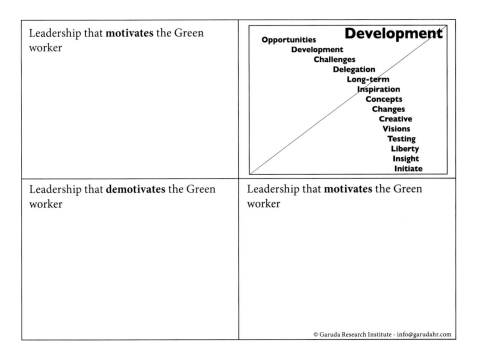

| Integration<br>**Understanding**<br>**Togetherness**<br>**Environment**<br>**Considerate**<br>**Involvement**<br>**Encourage**<br>**Fellowship**<br>**Harmony**<br>**Patience**<br>**Mediate**<br>**Values**<br>**Helpful**<br>**Trust**<br>**Unity** | Leadership that **motivates** the Blue worker |
|---|---|
| Leadership that **motivates** the Blue worker | Leadership that **demotivates** the blue worker<br><br><br><br><br><br>© Garuda Research Institute - info@garudahr.com |

| Leadership that **motivates** the Green worker | **Development**<br>**Opportunities**<br>**Development**<br>**Challenges**<br>**Delegation**<br>**Long-term**<br>**Inspiration**<br>**Concepts**<br>**Changes**<br>**Creative**<br>**Visions**<br>**Testing**<br>**Liberty**<br>**Insight**<br>**Initiate** |
|---|---|
| Leadership that **demotivates** the Green worker | Leadership that **motivates** the Green worker<br><br><br><br><br>© Garuda Research Institute - info@garudahr.com |

The Leader's Mental Scorecard. © Finn Havaleschka.

## Document 14: Analyzing the Current Situation

What type of requirements do you need to comply with in the situation you are in right now?

| Integration Needs: | Development Needs: |
|---|---|
| | |
| **Baser Needs:** | **Result Needs::** |
| | |

# Document 15: Current Focus Requirements

| | *In your role as manager and the daily decisions you make, I/we feel that the following is something that you should consider:* | Much more important | More important | Ok | Less important | Much less important | Priority |
|---|---|---|---|---|---|---|---|
| 1 | Helping and supporting others who are in difficulty and/or have a hard time managing | | | | | | |
| 2 | Organizing things so that your subordinates can do their work thoroughly and systematically | | | | | | |
| 3 | Acting and being perceived as an active, energetic and goal-oriented leader | | | | | | |
| 4 | Leading the way when changes have to be made | | | | | | |
| 5 | Formulating clear guidelines for subordinates' responsibilities and work performance | | | | | | |
| 6 | Creating a work environment with room and time for being social and making small talk | | | | | | |
| 7 | Inspiring subordinates to come up with creative solutions | | | | | | |
| 8 | Ensuring that everyone always utilizes time and other resources efficiently and in a targeted manner | | | | | | |
| 9 | Encouraging, praising, supporting and motivating all coworkers | | | | | | |
| 10 | Having systems so it's easy to see how far along people are in the work schedule/plans | | | | | | |
| 11 | Leading the way in working efficiently and targeted | | | | | | |
| 12 | Ensuring subordinates have the space, facilities and opportunity to solve problems independently | | | | | | |
| 13 | Making decisions based on clear and certain facts | | | | | | |
| 14 | Knowing what the background, values and attitudes of your subordinates are | | | | | | |
| 15 | Playing a vital role in the development of concepts and strategies | | | | | | |
| 16 | People do not waste time, but concentrate on creating visible results and getting things done | | | | | | |
| 17 | Mediating and unifying when different opinions and interests could cause conflict | | | | | | |
| 18 | Having systems that create structure, order and discipline in subordinates' activities | | | | | | |
| 19 | Ensuring that there is always a certain degree of competition among your subordinates | | | | | | |
| 20 | Being a source of inspiration and creative partner for subordinates | | | | | | |
| 21 | Directing and monitoring important tasks until completion | | | | | | |
| 22 | Creating a positive, open and trusting environment | | | | | | |
| 23 | Making long-term goals clear and comprehensible to everyone | | | | | | |
| 24 | Being more direct, concrete and definite if results fail to appear | | | | | | |

The Leader's Mental Scorecard. © Finn Havaleschka.

# Document 16: Mental Scorecard for Photocopying

| Situa-tion | Leader color | © Garuda Research Institute - info@garudahr.com<br><br>**Focus, week          and** | + | – |
|---|---|---|---|---|
| **1** | | **Action:** | | |
| | | Evaluate your ability to focus on and carry out this action. | | |
| **2** | | **Action:** | | |
| | | Evaluate your ability to focus on and carry out this action. | | |
| **3** | | **Action:** | | |
| | | Evaluate your ability to focus on and carry out this action. | | |
| **4** | | **Action:** | | |
| | | Evaluate your ability to focus on and carry out this action. | | |
| **5** | | **Action:** | | |
| | | Evaluate your ability to focus on and carry out this action. | | |
| **6** | | **Action:** | | |
| | | Evaluate your ability to focus on and carry out this action. | | |
| | | **Result for the 14 days** | | |
| | | **Ideal Score  (6 actions at 2 points each** | 12 | |
| | | **Your Mental Management Handicap** | | |

The Leader's Mental Scorecard. © Finn Havaleschka.

# List of Literature

Challoner, J. *The Brain*. London: Macmillan Publishers Ltd., 2000.

Harung H., Heaton D., and Alexander C., *"A Unified Theory of Leadership: experiences of higher states of consciousness in world-class leaders"*; Leadership and Organization Development Journal Vol. 16, No. 7, 1996, MCB University Press, Bradford, UK. p. 36-47.

Havaleschka, Finn. *The Successful Manager – How Do We Know*. Risskov, Denmark: Garuda Research Institute, 2002.

Havaleschka Finn. *Lederens vej fra viden til visdom*. Risskov, Denmark: Garuda Forlag, 1990.

Havaleschka, Finn. *On… Development, Life and Leadership*. Risskov, Denmark: Garuda Forlag, 1997.

Havaleschka, Finn. *Where Did the Development Go*. Risskov, Denmark: Garuda Research Institute, 2002.

Havaleschka, Finn. *Golferens Mentale Scorekort*. Risskov, Denmark: Garuda Forlag, 2003.

Kegan, R. *In Our Mental Heads: The Mental Demands of Modern Life*. Cambridge, MA: Harvard University Press, 1994.

Leonard, G. "Abraham Maslow and the New Self." *Esquire*, December 1983: p. 329-346.

Loevinger, J. *Ego Development: Conceptions and Theories*. New York, NY: Van Nostrand Reinhold, 1976.

Maslow, Abraham. *Toward a Psychology of Being*. New York, NY: Van Nostrand Reinhold, 1968.

Murray, J. E. *Motivationspsykologi*, Copenhagen, Denmark: Hans Reitzel, 1971.

Kerstin U. Moberg, *The Oxytocin Factor* (Cambridge, MA: Da Capo Press, 2003.

Nyborg, H. *Køn, Hormoner og Samfund*. Copenhagen, Denmark: Dansk Psykologisk Forlag, 1997.

Pervin, L. A. and John, O.P. *Personality, Theory and Research*. New York, NY: John Wiley & Sons, Inc., 1997.

Ridley, Matthew. *Genome: The Autobiography of a Species in 23 Chapters*. New York, NY: HarperCollins, 1999.

Rimpoche, Akong. Quoted from *"I didn't want to be rich (just enough to re-upholster the couch)"*, Smallbone M. and Shilkin A., Thin Rich Press 1993, p. 52.

Sitchin, Z. *The Twelfth Planet*. Santa Fe, New Mexico: Bear & Company, 1976.

# List of Proverbs – sentences

True insanity is….
using the same behavior and expecting different results.
>   *Einstein*

Before you try to change others to suit their behavior to your own, as a start try changing your behavior to suit the behavior of others.[47]

Knowing what's right is one thing.
Doing the right thing is another.
>   *Line from the movie "Horse whisper"*

I've had many troubles in my life,
most of which never happened.
>   *Mark Twain*

Where we feel safest and most secure,
that's where we want to stay.

You have to dare to lose your foothold to move forward.
>   *Soeren Kierkegaard*

The only way to free yourself of one thought
is to replace it with another one.

Before other people tune into what you are saying or your ideas,
they tune into your aura.

What you see is in the eye of the beholder.

Sometimes we have to let go so that we can hold on.

Your strength is also your weakness.

---

[47] If nothing else is stated you can find these sentences or proverbs in this book or in my book: *On…. Development,Life and Leadership.*

Motivation comes from that joy one takes
in advance in the expectation of success.

How many times have you said no to happiness
because it came from the wrong corner?

No one, not even your children, is born into this world
to satisfy your expectations.

If there is a doubt, there is no doubt.
*Line from the movie "Ronin"*

In principle I do nothing wrong.
I simply learn to do the right things too slowly.

We are and become what we think,
and get the opportunities that our thoughts open for us.

What you do not in advance imagine in your mental world,
you will have difficulty carrying out in the real world.

We have to change our patterns of reacting to experience.
For our problems do not lie in what we experience,
but in the attitude we have towards it.
*Akong Rimpoche*

Where man build on false grounds,
the more he build, the greater the ruin.
*Thomas Hobbes, Leviathan*

# Coaching: The Software and coaching concept

On the basis of the methods presented in this book, Garuda has developed a software program for use by professional human resources consultants and managers interested in coaching. The program contains the original tests and questionnaires (which are somewhat longer and more extensive than the ones you will see in this book), together with a systematic collection and processing of data aimed at determining a leader's focus and focusing needs.

The program also helps coaches and leaders identify the leadership actions specified in the Leader's Mental Scorecard that will teach them to act in accordance with the situation or with the needs of a coworker.

The result is coworkers who are better satisfied and more motivated, and flexible leadership that allows each worker to apply their full intellectual, mental and physical resources to their work and thus to achieving results. To learn more about the program, and the possibilities for you to become a Certified Mental Scorecard Coach, please contact Garuda Research Institute by telephone at (country code 45) 8746-8600 or by e-mail at finn@garuda.dk

## Illustrations

We have installed all the illustrations of the four types presented in this book on a CD. If you are interested in using the illustrations in your activities, you can purchase the CD from the Garuda Research Institute. Please send a mail to info@garudahr.com or go to www.mental-scorecard.com.